>>

Career
Excellence

>>

Peter M. Hess

ADAPTED BY LEO SEVIGNY

THOMSON

DELMAR LEARNING   Australia Canada Mexico Singapore Spain United Kingdom United States

Career Excellence
Peter M. Hess

Vice President, Career Education Strategic Business Unit:
Dawn Gerrain

Director of Editorial:
Sherry Gomoll

Acquisitions Editor:
Martine Edwards

Developmental Editor:
Gerald O'Malley

Editorial Assistant:
Jennifer Anderson

Director of Production:
Wendy A. Troeger

Production Manager:
J. P. Henkel

Production Editor:
Nina Tucciarelli

Director of Marketing:
Wendy E. Mapstone

Channel Manager:
Gerard McAvey

For permission to use material from the text or product, submit a request online at http://www.thomsonrights.com

Any additional questions about permissions can be submitted by email to thomsonrights@thomson.com

Library of Congress Cataloging-in-Publication Data
Hess, Peter M.
  Career excellence / Peter M. Hess ; adapted by Leo Sevigny.
    p. cm.

  Includes bibliographical references and index.
  ISBN-13: 978-1-4018-8201-3
1. Job hunting. 2. Career changes. 3. Vocational guidance. I. Sevigny, Leo. II. Title.
HF5382.7.H48 2006
650.14—dc22   2005008762

NOTICE TO THE READER

Publisher does not warrant or guarantee any of the products described herein or perform any independent analysis in connection with any of the product information contained herein. Publisher does not assume, and expressly disclaims, any obligation to obtain and include information other than that provided to it by the manufacturer.

The reader is expressly warned to consider and adopt all safety precautions that might be indicated by the activities herein and to avoid all potential hazards. By following the instructions contained herein, the reader willingly assumes all risks in connection with such instructions.

The Publisher makes no representation or warranties of any kind, including but not limited to, the warranties of fitness for particular purpose or merchantability, nor are any such representations implied with respect to the material set forth herein, and the publisher takes no responsibility with respect to such material. The publisher shall not be liable for any special, consequential, or exemplary damages resulting, in whole or part, from the readers' use of, or reliance upon, this material.

A special thanks to my Mom and Dad for their encouragement, courage, patience, inspiration, and for being my best friends. You are the reason for my success. Thank you.

Contents at a Glance

>>

Contents

Before any major life change, especially a career change, one must take stock of his or her own values, beliefs, and motivators in order to reach set goals. *Career Excellence* is a comprehensive guide for those preparing to change careers. Unlike any other book of its kind, this guide takes the reader from the initial stages of making a career change to landing the job, to success in the workplace. *Career Excellence* not only presents the information and tools necessary to begin a job search—how-tos on updating a resume, creating a winning cover letter, preparing a portfolio, and kicking off the job search—it also covers career excellence once the reader lands the job. It advises on how to excel on the job by making decisions based on inner drive, and includes tips on how to excel with new colleagues, how to impress the boss while maintaining integrity, how to build alliances, and how to continue to make decisions with honesty and consistency. Designed to help readers focus on their internal drive for initiating a successful job search, this unique resource will help them change careers with an organized approach and with an opportunity for self-exploration.

PETER M. HESS is a successful entrepreneur who has founded many very successful start-ups, and helped tens of thousands of young adult professionals achieve their career goals.

Introduction

>>>

Whether you are searching for your ideal job or are satisfied with the position you have, today's rapidly changing workplace requires constant personal and professional development. Savvy employees and job seekers understand the need to be prepared for inevitable changes in corporate structure, new job opportunities, and personal lifestyle. The *Pathway to Excellence* series is for anyone looking to build a foundation of effective communication skills, job search techniques, and a personal success plan for growth and promotion in any industry.

The series delivers real-life skills and strategies that can be applied immediately to your personal or professional life. This book provides a comprehensive guide for success when read cover to cover. The straightforward approach of the text also makes it an excellent reference if you have limited time and need specific advice by topic.

Icons used throughout the book help to highlight key points and exercises.

 Exercises for you to complete

 A helpful perspective on how to accomplish the goal at hand

 A list of common mistakes to be on the lookout for

 A summary of the main points of each chapter

However you make use of the insights in this series, our hope is that you continue to pursue your individual path to excellence.

Chapter 1

Success as a Path of Life

You don't need a crystal ball to predict the successful future that awaits you. By knowing two things—who you are and what you want—you are primed to enjoy a successful life. With that knowledge, you can create your successful life by imagining a vision of the future, formulating a plan of action to get there, and enacting your plan with specific steps. This chapter will help you to accomplish those vital tasks.

> The best way to predict the future is to create it.
> PETER F. DRUCKER,
> ECONOMIST,
> JOURNALIST,
> AND AUTHOR

After completing this chapter, you should understand

> ➤ the essence of success.
> ➤ the values, beliefs, and self-belief that have made you the person you are.
> ➤ your deepest dreams and wishes and how they can become the foundation for your goals.
> ➤ how to set goals and develop an action plan to achieve those goals.
> ➤ how to overcome success barriers.
> ➤ how to monitor your progress on the path to success.

Defining Success

According to the French novelist Alexandre Dumas, "Nothing succeeds like success." But what exactly is success? Some people believe that wealth or fame are hallmarks of success. For others, though, success is measured not by one's net worth but by one's self-worth.

These individuals feel positive about themselves and feel fulfilled in all areas of their lives. They seize each new day as an opportunity to grow and to develop to their greatest potential. They view success not as transitory stopping points but as a path that winds through life. And they are successful. Their secret?

They know who they are and what they want. They define success for themselves, create a vision of the future, and construct a plan of action to get there. They enact their plan of action by putting one foot in front of the other on their life's path and begin their journey of a thousand miles.

Do you know who you are? Do you know what you want to accomplish? The answers to these questions can be found through self-discovery.

Discovering Who You Are: Your Values

Research shows that successful people live by a set of values. Values are your core thoughts and feelings about yourself and about life, which lead you to make decisions and to act in certain ways based on those thoughts and feelings. For example, you may identify with the value of honesty. If so, you will tell the truth because you think that lying is wrong. You will feel betrayed when a person you trust lies to you. You will take action to correct a mistake rather than cover up the error or blame someone else.

These three aspects of values—thoughts, feelings, and actions—are meant to operate harmoniously. But sometimes one or more aspects are in conflict. If someone invites you to an event that you don't want to attend, you might decide to lie and say that you've already made plans to go somewhere else that day. Afterward you will probably feel uncomfortable because your feeling that lying is wrong is at odds with your action of telling a lie. Research shows that people feel best when all three aspects of their values are in harmony.

You acquired your values during childhood through the influences of your family and friends, your religion and your cultural heritage, and through the influences of school, the media, and modern society. But you may not be consciously aware of the range of values that have formed you as a person.

Awareness of your values increases your understanding of yourself and the level of satisfaction you feel when you make decisions. You can achieve this awareness through values clarification, a process that involves choosing, prizing, and acting on your values. To get a sense of this process complete the following exercises.

One of the challenges of determining your values is to bring your thoughts about the many motivations and directions for life into focus. It can be difficult to condense years of life into a series of phrases or ideas. Though difficult, keep in mind that your values are most likely going to change throughout your life, so do not focus on finding exact and permanent answers to the following exercises. The best you can do is to determine what your prevalent values at this point in your life are. By creating a snapshot of your current values, you will be better able to direct your life and the major decisions you are about to make.

YOUR TURN

My Values—Part 1

Purpose: To identify your values and to determine what is important to you.

Following is an alphabetical list of fifteen values. Review the list then rank the importance of each value to you in ascending order. Place a 1 next to the value that is the most important to you, and place a 15 next to the value that is the least important to you. Consider your rankings carefully and spend enough time on this exercise so that the rankings accurately reflect your values.

Value	Rank
Ambition	
Autonomy	
Cheerfulness	
Competence (being capable)	
Courteousness (being well-mannered)	
Forgiveness	
Helpfulness (working for the welfare of others)	
Honesty	
Being Logical	
Obedience (being dutiful, respectful)	

(continued)

Value	Rank
Open-mindedness	_____
Recognition	_____
Being Responsible	_____
Being Self-controlled (committed)	_____
Wisdom	_____

My Values—Part 2

Purpose: To choose your values and to determine what is most important to you.

Review your list of value rankings in Part 1 and then complete the statements that follow.

1. The value rankings that I am satisfied with are:

_____

_____

_____

_____

2. The value rankings that I am dissatisfied with are:

_____

_____

_____

_____

Consider what you have learned about your values by completing these exercises. Then record in the following table your five most important values, your five somewhat important values, and your five least important values. You can use this rank-ordered list to remind yourself of your values and to use these values in making decisions.

Most Important

1. _____

2. _____

3. _____

4._____

5._____

Somewhat Important

1._____

2._____

3._____

4._____

5._____

Least Important

1._____

2._____

3._____

4._____

5._____

My Values—Part 3

Purpose: To prize your values and to identify potential rewards that can be used as motivators.

Use the space provided to list twenty activities that you love. These activities can be big or small, ones that you do indoors, outdoors, by yourself, or with others. Be specific when listing the activities (e.g., reading mystery novels). When you finish your list, complete the statements that follow.

Twenty Activities I Love to Do

1._____

2._____

3._____

4._____

5._____

6._____

7._____

8._____

9._____

10._____

11._____

12._____

13._____

14._____

15._____

16._____

17._____

18._____

19._____

20._____

Review your list of activities and then complete the following statements.

I have identified the following patterns in the activities that I love to do:

_____

_____

_____

_____

_____

_____

The aspects that please me the most about this list are:

_____

_____

_____

_____

_____

_____

_____

From this exercise I learned the following about myself:

_____

_____

_____

_____

_____

_____

_____

Three values that are suggested by my list of activities are:

1._____

2._____

3._____

Five activities on my list that I have not done within the last six months are:

1._____

2._____

3._____

4._____

5._____

Five activities on my list that I can use to motivate myself are:

1. _____

2. _____

3. _____

4. _____

5. _____

My Values—Part 4

Purpose: To evaluate the consistency of the harmony between your actions and your values.

From the Part 4 exercise, record your five most important values. Then, for the next week keep a written record of the actions you take to support your values. For example, if one of your most important values is being helpful, you would record actions such as volunteering for a community cleanup committee or sending a journal article to a colleague.

My Most Important Values Are:

1. _____

2. _____

3. _____

4. _____

5. _____

Discovering Who You Are: Your Beliefs

You discovered that values are at the center of your thoughts and feelings about yourself and about life. Your values may guide your decisions—to act in a certain way based on your thoughts and feelings. Growing from your values are attitudes about yourself, other people, situations, objects, or ideas. These attitudes are your beliefs. For example, if one of your values is being helpful or working for the welfare of others, you may believe that you should volunteer time to your community's food pantry.

Your beliefs have a powerful impact on your behavior. Although you may be unaware of this interplay, your beliefs—both positive and negative—affect how you behave. Negative beliefs, such as "I can't do math," limit your behavior. If you truly believe that you can't do math, you don't put forth the needed effort to try to understand mathematical concepts, and as a result you fail. In effect, the belief comes true because you believe it to be so. Psychologists call this a self-fulfilling prophecy.

Self-fulfilling prophecy also works with positive beliefs. In fact, positive beliefs are just as powerful as negative beliefs. The difference is that positive beliefs—"I can find a job I love" or "I will complete that important project"— spur you to action and stimulate you to make progress. They allow you to focus on an objective, take the steps needed to achieve that goal, and pursue that target with persistence and confidence.

You can harness the power of positive beliefs by using a technique called *positive self-talk*. This is a way to silence that negative inner voice that undermines your chances for success. The niggling negative voice is like an audiotape, playing the same message over and over again in your mind. Positive self-talk, also called affirmations, enables you to "erase" the old, negative messages and to "record" new, positive messages that you can listen to every day. The new messages use I statements in the present tense, focus on what could be, and include positive action: "I like who I am and the successful direction in which I'm headed." Because thought comes before action, affirmations ready your mind to create circumstances that will help you reach your goals.

Use the following exercises to identify your negative beliefs, turn them into positive beliefs, and then use them as affirmations.

My Beliefs

Purpose: To identify negative beliefs and transform them into positive beliefs.

Use the space provided to list five negative beliefs you have about yourself that you think have affected your behavior. For example, "I am a boring person. No one would be interested in me."

1. _____

2. _____

3. _____

4. _____

5. _____

Psychologist and philosopher William James recommended that: "If you want a quality, act as if you already had it." Use the space provided to rewrite your negative beliefs into positive beliefs. Remember to use I statements in the present tense, focus on what could be, and include a positive action. For example, "I am an interesting person, and I look forward to meeting new people."

1. _____

2. _____

3. _____

4. _____

5. _____

My Affirmations

Purpose: To transform positive beliefs into affirmations and to put them into daily practice.

An easy way to begin using affirmations is to choose a simple aspect of your life that you would like to see changed. For example, "I have trouble finishing projects on time." In the space provided, write one aspect of your life that you would like to change.

_____

_____

_____

_____

_____

_____

Next, picture in your mind how you will act when you change this aspect of your life. Then, write an I statement that is positive, uses present tense, and focuses on the change. For example: "I enjoy finishing each project in a timely manner." In the following space, write your affirmation.

_____

_____

_____

_____

_____

_____

Erasing negative mental messages requires repetition of your positive mental message. Choose one of these two methods: (1) Write your affirmation on paper, or (2) read your affirmation aloud. Then enact your chosen method at least ten times each day for the next two weeks. In the following space, write the method you plan to use.

_____

_____

_____

_____

_____

_____

At the end of two weeks, describe in the following space your experience with your affirmation. Did it change your actions? Compare how you felt two weeks ago and how you feel now.

_____

_____

_____

_____

_____

_____

Discovering Who You Are: Your Self-Belief

You've identified your values and clarified your beliefs. The combination of your values and your beliefs is your self-belief. Psychologists define self-belief as a person's confidence in and respect for his or her own abilities. If you have a strong self-belief, you know who you are and what you value, and you can triumph over any adversity. Use the following exercise to evaluate your self-belief.

YOUR TURN

My Self-Belief

Purpose: To describe your current self-belief and to envision your future self-belief.

Complete the following statements on your personality traits in the space provided. Personality traits include qualities such as being ambitious, considerate, gloomy, insensitive, motivated, outgoing, passive, quiet, etc.

Right now, I see myself as having the following personality traits:

_____

_____

_____

_____

_____

_____

In the future, I hope to have the following personality traits:

_____

_____

_____

_____

_____

_____

Your Basis for Success

Your self-belief is your basis for success. Believing in yourself allows you to use all of your potential to take action. When you take action, you make progress and achieve results. Achieving results strengthens your self-belief because of the sense of accomplishment. With a strengthened self-belief, you gain the confidence to be bolder in your actions. Being bolder in your actions boosts your self-belief. You could think of this system as a power wheel with four linking components: potential leads to action, action leads to results, and results leads to self-belief. Once you allow your power wheel to begin rolling, there's no telling what you can accomplish or where you can go.

Determining What You Want to Accomplish: Your Dreams

Now that you've considered your values, beliefs, and self-belief, you have discovered who you are. The next step is to determine what you want to accomplish during your life. One way to do this is to think about your dreams.

What is your fondest dream? Do you long to launch your own business? Do you aspire to elected public office? Do you yearn to become a fashion designer? Spinning dreams is often called building castles in the air. Many people stop there, but successful people construct foundations for their dreams. You can do this, too. Complete the following exercise to get in touch with your deepest dreams and wishes.

YOUR TURN

My Dreams

Purpose: To identify your dreams and wishes.

Imagine that you have only one year left to live. Use the space provided to describe how you would spend those last 12 months.

_____

_____

_____

_____

_____

_____

A genie magically materializes before you and grants you three wishes. What do you wish for?

1._____

2._____

3._____

A wizard waves a magic wand and guarantees you success in anything you do. What is the one thing you most want to do?

_____

_____

_____

_____

_____

_____

Review your answers to the questions in this exercise. Do your answers reveal a pattern? Does a specific goal appear consistently among the three previous scenarios? What do you observe when you compare all of your answers? Note those observations in the space provided.

_____

_____

_____

_____

_____

_____

_____

_____

_____

_____

_____

_____

_____

Determining What You Want to Accomplish: Your Goals

Your dreams can be the springboard for many of your goals. Goals come in various shapes and sizes. You probably have personal, educational, professional, and community goals. Within the scope of this book, you'll have an opportunity to concentrate on professional goals.

Professional goals are the objectives for your career. These objectives can be broad-based—"I want to earn a competitive wage"—or narrowly focused—"I want to acquire a professional pilot's license."

In setting professional goals, strive to be realistic, considering your unique talents and attributes. For example, you may wish to be a dancer on Broadway. But if you have short legs and two left feet, your goal is unrealistic. You can waste much energy trying to reach an unrealistic goal, or you can channel that energy into another aspect of that goal—one that is more realistic for you. In addition to making your goals realistic, you will want to be sure they'll take some effort to achieve. Easily attained goals that fail to challenge you don't allow you to reach your full potential.

Another consideration for the goals you set is the length of time required to achieve them. Short-term goals can be attained in one year or less. Intermediate-term goals can be attained in one to five years. Long-term goals can take five years or longer to attain.

The time commitment necessary for intermediate- and long-term goals often discourages people from setting any goals at all. This needn't happen to you, if you have the right mind-set. For example, your long-term goal may be to earn a doctorate on a part-time basis, and you estimate that this will take ten years. Break down this long-term goal into a series of short-term goals. View each course you take as a short-term goal contributing to your long-term objective. After you've thought about your professional goals, commit those goals to paper. Research shows that individuals who write out their goals are more likely to achieve them than people who fail to jot them down.

When recording your goals, bear in mind these strategies:

> *Set a variety of realistic goals.* Having a number of goals with varying time commitments—short-term and long-term—in different areas of your life—personal, professional, educational—will allow you to maintain balance. But be realistic. Don't set so many goals that you become frustrated when you can't achieve them all.

- *Choose goals that are yours.* Well-intentioned people in your life may encourage you to set goals that are unrealistic or just plain wrong for you. Make sure your goals spring from your dreams so that you'll feel satisfaction in achieving them.
- *Use positive language.* Write "I will accept a job with a company that offers a mentoring program," rather than "I won't take a job unless the company offers a mentoring program."
- *Be specific.* Write "I would like to visit Italy," rather than "I want to take a trip."
- *Make your goals measurable.* You could write "I want to lose weight." But how will you know that you've attained your goal? After 5 pounds? After 25 pounds? You need a method by which you measure whether you've achieved your goal. You make your goals measurable when you answer these questions: What is to be accomplished? At what point will I know that I have accomplished it? "I want to lose 15 pounds" is a measurable goal.
- *Establish a deadline.* What is the time frame for achieving your goal? Whether you want to attain the goal in six months or in six years, set a start date and an end date.
- *Remember the nature of goals.* Your goals will change, so it's important to reassess your goals on a regular basis as you grow, change, and develop.

Use the exercise on the following pages to identify your professional goals and the time commitments necessary for you to achieve them.

YOUR TURN

My Goals

Purpose: To record your professional goals and to classify your goals as *short-term* (one year or less to accomplish), *intermediate-term* (one to five years to accomplish), or *long-term* (more than five years to accomplish). In the space provided, write up to five short-, intermediate-, and long-term goals.

Professional Goals
Short-Term

1._____

2._____

3._____

4._____

5._____

Intermediate-Term

1._____

2._____

3._____

4._____

5._____

Long-Term

1._____

2._____

3._____

4._____

5._____

Formulating Your Action Plan

Ahead of you is a journey of a thousand miles. Since you want to arrive by the most direct route, you might consider using a map to lessen the chances of getting lost along the way. "Begin with the end in mind," according to Stephen R. Covey, the author of *The Seven Habits of Highly Effective People.*

So after you've decided on your destination—your goal—create a map or an action plan to plot out exactly how you will arrive at your objective.

Reflect on a long-term goal first; state your goal specifically and indicate a time frame for accomplishing it. Next, break down the long-term goal into a number of short-term objectives—or steps—that will lead you to achieving the long-term goal. To monitor your progress, list specific results and establish deadlines for each short-term objective.

Here's an example: Perhaps you want to open your own public relations firm, and you decide to accomplish this within seven years. With that in mind, you plan the various steps that you must take in order to launch the firm. The steps include: (1) gaining experience by working in a small public relations company for five years; (2) taking business courses at night to acquire accounting, management, and marketing skills; (3) saving 10 percent of your annual salary each year for five years to be used for start-up expenses; (4) obtaining a job after five years in a large public relations company to gain more specialized knowledge; and (5) saving 15 percent of your annual salary for the last two years to be used for living expenses after you open your firm. In the exercise that follows, choose three of your most important long-term goals and create an action plan to help you achieve those goals.

 YOUR TURN

My Action Plan

Purpose: To focus on three important long-term goals and to create an action plan that leads to attainment of those goals.

1. Long-Term Goal:_____

   To be accomplished by:_____

   *Step 1:*_____
   Results needed: _____
   To be accomplished by:_____

   *Step 2:*_____
   Results needed: _____
   To be accomplished by:_____

Step 3: _____
Results needed: _____
To be accomplished by: _____

Step 4: _____
Results needed: _____
To be accomplished by: _____

2. Long-Term Goal: _____
To be accomplished by: _____

Step 1: _____
Results needed: _____
To be accomplished by: _____

Step 2: _____
Results needed: _____
To be accomplished by: _____

Step 3: _____
Results needed: _____
To be accomplished by: _____

Step 4: _____
Results needed: _____
To be accomplished by: _____

3. Long-Term Goal: _____
To be accomplished by: _____

Step 1: _____
Results needed: _____
To be accomplished by: _____

Step 2: _____
Results needed: _____
To be accomplished by: _____

Step 3: _____

Results needed: _____

To be accomplished by: _____

Step 4: _____

Results needed: _____

To be accomplished by: _____

Following Your Path to Success

Once you've completed your detailed action plan, you can begin your journey. The plan will keep you on track, but you must work hard to make progress, remain focused on your goals, and keep moving even when you encounter potholes and roadblocks.

Procrastination is one type of pothole. Rather than doing it now, a person puts off a task until later. That is the shortest route to failure. To overcome procrastination:

> ➤ *Set a start date.* This will allow you to get ready to begin once you have made a commitment to yourself.
> ➤ *Make a list of tiny tasks.* Tiny tasks take a mere minute or two, give you a sense of accomplishment, and enable you to begin.
> ➤ *Work for 15 minutes.* Select a short period of time during each day when you accomplish tasks relating to your goal.
> ➤ *Tackle the hardest part first.* Once you have the hardest or the worst part behind you, the path to achieving the goal becomes smoother.

Chapter 5 provides additional tips for combating procrastination. If the pothole of procrastination doesn't stop you, the roadblock of fear sometimes does. Fear of failure and fear of success are both barriers to action.

Fear of failure often results when a person is afraid of appearing incompetent. The person views failure as defeat instead of considering that failure is only a temporary setback from which valuable lessons can be learned. According to psychologist B. F. Skinner, "A failure is not always a mistake, it may simply be the best one can do under the circumstances. The real mistake is to stop trying."

An effective way to bring values, beliefs, and goals together is to create a statement of Personal Vision. A Personal Vision statement brings together these elements into a motivational statement that you can use to center yourself in your own belief system. Burgess, Pugh, and Sevigny in *Great Explorations— The Personal Vision Statement Workbook* discuss the process by comparing it to a personal voyage that you take to give yourself direction and motivation. To begin, select your five core values from the above exercises and create a statement that encapsulates your defined belief systems. You can then use this statement to assist you in your decision-making processes. ▪

Fear of success often results when a person is afraid of new situations or responsibilities that success promises. The person views these changes as ones they don't deserve or ones they are incapable of handling. Successful writer, activist, and educator Audre Lorde said, "When I dare to be powerful—to use my strength in the service of my vision, then it becomes less and less important whether I am afraid."

To overcome fear:

> *Make a list of what makes you afraid.* Then create affirmations to counteract each item on your list.
> *Collect success stories.* Read about prominent people who experienced failure. From their stories, study how these individuals rose above failure and triumphed.
> *Write your own success stories.* Begin keeping a success journal, detailing each time you achieve something special, no matter how small. When you feel afraid, read through your journal and gain strength from the knowledge that, despite your fears, you are successful. Maybe you are fortunate in not being halted by potholes and roadblocks as you follow your path to success. In fact, you may be chugging along at a good clip for a long stretch of time. Then, suddenly, you find yourself on a plateau with nothing much happening. The phenomenon of plateauing— making rapid progress then leveling out—is normal. Keep plugging away, and before you know it, you'll feel the beginnings of another spurt of progress.

To keep yourself going when you hit a plateau:

> *Keep your energy level high.* Repeat affirmations. Create special affirmations to help you cope with your plateau period. Practice visualization or the art of forming in your mind a picture of your goal. Visualize what it will be like when your goal is attained.
> *Praise yourself.* Reflect on the distance you've already covered and congratulate yourself on your accomplishments.
> *Reward yourself.* For each step toward a goal, treat yourself to something you enjoy. Use some of the motivators you discovered in the exercise *My Values—Part 3*.
> *Share your successes with family and friends.* Tell the people in your life about your goals and what you have achieved so far. Not only will they congratulate you, but the pride reflected in their smiles and the good wishes they extend to you will act as powerful motivators to keep you going.

How Close Are You to Success?

According to Thomas Edison, "Many of life's failures are people who did not realize how close they were to success when they gave up." By monitoring the attainment of your short-term goals, you will know how close you are to successfully achieving your long-term goals. But keep in mind that circumstances sometimes cause goals to shift and to change. So you may find it helpful to obtain periodic feedback on the progress you are making. Use the following exercise to generate action plan feedback.

YOUR TURN

Action Plan Feedback

Purpose: To obtain feedback and evaluation of strategies for attaining goals.

Periodically, check your progress along the path to evaluate how you are doing. This feedback will help you to decide whether your action plan is progressing smoothly or you need to make course corrections. Focusing on one of your goals at a time, complete each statement using the space provided:

To date, I have accomplished:

_____

_____

_____

_____

_____

_____

The parts I liked were:

_____

_____

_____

_____

_____

_____

The parts I didn't like were:

_____

_____

_____

_____

_____

_____

I forgot to include the following steps:

_____

_____

_____

_____

_____

_____

I will change or adjust the following:

_____

_____

_____

_____

_____

_____

Regarding the time frame, I need to make the following adjustment:

_____

_____

_____

_____

_____

_____

 ## *ELEMENTS OF EXCELLENCE*

As you come to the end of this chapter, reflect on the journey of a thousand miles that you began with the process of self-discovery.

> ➤ You discovered who you are—your values, beliefs, and self-belief.
> ➤ You discovered what you want to accomplish—your dreams and goals.
> ➤ You created an action plan and learned how to follow the path to success by overcoming procrastination and fear and by keeping yourself going when you hit a plateau.
> ➤ You also discovered how to tell how close you are to the success you envision.

Don't stop there. Step into Chapter 2 where you'll focus on success in the job search—your next step on your journey of a thousand miles. ■

Read All About It!

Bristol, Claude M. *The Magic of Believing: The Science of Setting Your Goal and Then Reaching It.* New York: Simon & Schuster, 1992.

Carter, Carol, Gary Izumo, & Sarah Lyman Kravits. *The Career Tool Kit: Skills for Success.* Upper Saddle River, NJ: Prentice Hall, 1997.

Covey, Stephen R. *The Seven Habits of Highly Effective People.* New York: Simon & Schuster, 1989.

Dean, Amy E., & Dan Olmos. *Lifegoals: Setting & Achieving Goals to Chart the Course of Your Life.* Carlsbad, CA: Hay House, 1991.

Driggers, Joann. *Life Management Skills: Taking Charge of Your Future.* Clifton Park, NY: Delmar Learning, 1999.

Gale, Linda. *Discover What You're Best At: A Complete Career System That Lets You Test Yourself to Discover Your Own True Career Capabilities.* New York: Fireside, 1998.

Greeson, Gene. *Goal Setting: Turning Your Mountains into Molehills.* St. Charles, MO: Potentials Unlimited, 1994.

Jarow, Rick. *Creating the Work You Love: Courage, Commitment and Career.* Rochester, VT: Inner Traditions International Ltd., 1995.

Leatz, Christine A., & Mary W. Stolar. *Career Success/Personal Success: How to Stay Healthy in a High Stress Environment.* New York: McGraw-Hill, 1992.

Peale, Norman Vincent, & Kenneth Blanchard. *The Power of Ethical Management.* New York: Fawcett, 1989.

Pitino, Rick, with Bill Reynolds. *Success Is a Choice: Ten Steps to Overachieving in Business and Life.* New York: Broadway Books, 1997.

Rouillard, Larrie A. *Goals and Goal Setting.* Los Altos, CA: Crisp Publications, 1998.

Simon, Sidney, Leland W. Howe, & Howard Kirschenbaum. *Values Clarification: A Handbook of Practical Strategies for Teachers and Students.* Chesterfield, MA: Values Press, 1978.

Throop, Robert K., & Marion B. Castellucci. *Reaching Your Potential: Personal and Professional Development,* 2nd ed. Clifton Park, NY: Delmar Learning, 1999.

Waitley, Denis. *The New Dynamics of Goal Setting: Flextactics for a Fast-Changing Future.* New York: William Morrow, 1997.

Wilson, Susan B. *Goal Setting (The Worksmart Series).* New York: AMACOM, 1994.

Books I've Read

Use the space provided to list the books you've read in this subject area and to reflect on what you've learned from reading them.

1. _____

2. _____

3. _____

4. _____

5. _____

Internet Resources

http://www.selfgrowth.com

> *Self-Improvement Online, Inc.* This Web site contains information on personal growth and provides links to other sites and newsgroups.

http://www.psychwww.com

> *Mind Tools Ltd.* This British company offers software that helps people achieve more productive thinking. Their Web site contains general advice on goal setting and suggestions for achieving goals.

My Favorite Internet Sites

Use the space provided to list your favorite Internet sites.

1. _____

2. _____

3. _____

4. _____

5. _____

Career Success Notes

_____

_____

_____

_____

_____

_____

_____

_____

_____

_____

_____

_____

_____

_____

_____

_____

_____

_____

_____

_____

_____

_____

Chapter 2

Success in the Job Search

Jobs don't find you. You find jobs. Find the right job successfully by setting a career objective; conducting a personalized job search complete with resumé, cover letter, and portfolio; and knowing how to attain and maintain a positive attitude. This chapter will help you to accomplish these vital tasks.

> Success doesn't come to you . . . you go to it.
>
> MARVA COLLINS,
> AMERICAN EDUCATOR

After completing this chapter, you should understand

> ➤ how to match yourself to a career and set a career objective.
> ➤ the components of a successful job search.
> ➤ how to develop a personalized job search.
> ➤ how to create a resumé, cover letter, and portfolio.
> ➤ the strategies for keeping a positive mental attitude.

Anthropologist Ashley Montagu said it in a nutshell: "It is work, work that one delights in, that is the surest guarantor of happiness." Wouldn't it be great to love your work? To use your abilities and interests to make a difference in the world? To be paid for doing a job that you're good at, a job that's fun?

A job? Fun? Yes! Knowing who you are and what you want to accomplish puts you on the fast track to challenging jobs and a satisfying career. Successful people know that work is play, and that's where the fun part comes in. No boring, dead-end jobs for you. By figuring out what you have to offer and what you want out of your future career, you'll be able to find jobs that are good matches for you, pull together an effective resumé and cover letter, and launch a personalized search for the right job—one that delights you and makes you happy.

At the Crossroads of Success

You are at the crossroads of success. The next steps you take will mean the difference between a job that just pays the bills and a career that pays off by giving you more than just a salary. Start by heading to your local library and looking at the *Occupational Outlook Handbook,* published by the U.S. Department of Labor's Bureau of Labor Statistics. You'll find information about employment trends, descriptions of hundreds of occupations, and sources of career guidance. You can also access the *Occupational Outlook Handbook* on-line at http://stats.bls.gov (click on "Publications and Research Papers").

Find out if your library has the periodical *Occupational Outlook Quarterly,* also published by the U.S. Department of Labor. You'll find up-to-date information about job market trends and predictions about the fastest-growing jobs within the hottest industries.

Your local library will also have resources about the educational requirements of various jobs. That information will help you decide if your current degree will open those job doors or if you'll be more successful by gaining further education.

Once you've learned about the job market and educational requirements for jobs, you can match yourself to a career. That process begins by looking at yourself—at your qualities and abilities.

Matching Yourself to a Career

Many people think they have no skills or abilities to offer prospective employers. They're wrong! You can prove it to yourself.

The U.S. Department of Labor compiled a list of personal qualities, foundation skills, and workplace skills that lead to top job performance in today's workplace. They apply to any type of career. For some jobs, though, you'll need more of some skills than others. How do you stack up? Scan the list and then complete the exercise that follows.

What You Need for Top Job Performance Today[1]

PERSONAL QUALITIES	Individual responsibility
	Self-belief
	Self-management
	Sociability
	Integrity

FOUNDATION SKILLS	**Basic Skills:**
	Reading
	Writing
	Arithmetic
	Mathematics
	Speaking
	Listening
	Thinking Skills:
	Ability to learn
	Reasoning
	Creative thinking
	Decision making
	Problem solving

RESOURCE SKILLS	Allocate time, money, materials, space, and staff

(continued)

INTERPERSONAL SKILLS	Work on teams
	Teach others
	Serve customers
	Lead
	Negotiate
	Work with people of diverse backgrounds
INFORMATION SKILLS	Acquire and evaluate data
	Organize and maintain files
	Interpret and communicate
	Use computers to process information
SYSTEMS SKILLS	Understand social, organizational, and technological systems
	Monitor and correct performance
	Design or improve systems
TECHNOLOGY SKILLS	Select equipment and tools
	Apply technology to specific tasks
	Maintain and troubleshoot equipment

[1]Source: U.S. Department of Labor, Secretary's Commission on Achieving Necessary Skills (SCANS), *Learning a Living: A Blueprint for High Performance*, Washington, DC, 1992, p. 3.

How I Stack Up

Purpose: To identify your skills and abilities.

For this exercise, refer to your answers in *My Values—Part 3* (p. 5). What are the five activities you most enjoy doing? Choose from those you enjoy at work, at home or in the community, during sports or recreation.

1._____

_____

2._____

_____

3._____

_____

4._____

_____

5._____

_____

Refer to the skills listed in "What You Need for Top Job Performance Today." Think about how you use those skills in the five activities you most enjoy doing. List those skills in the space provided.

Skills I Enjoy Using in Activity 1

_____

_____

_____

_____

_____

_____

Skills I Enjoy Using in Activity 2

_____

_____

_____

_____

_____

_____

Skills I Enjoy Using in Activity 3

_____

_____

_____

_____

_____

_____

Skills I Enjoy Using in Activity 4

_____

_____

_____

_____

_____

_____

Skills I Enjoy Using in Activity 5

_____

_____

_____

_____

_____

_____

Go back to the list in "What You Need for Top Job Performance Today." Circle all the qualities and skills that you just listed for each activity. How do you stack up? Write your answer in the space provided.

_____
_____
_____
_____
_____
_____
_____
_____
_____
_____
_____
_____
_____
_____

Beside qualities and skills, you also have education and experience to offer prospective employers. Your education shows that you have the ability to learn and demonstrates that you can read, write, and do computations. It also points to the body of knowledge you've gained in specific areas such as accounting, management, or computer information systems.

TIPS

Keep in mind that your other experiences are valuable, too. They include:

> full-time or part-time paid work.
> apprenticeships and internships.
> community, church, or other volunteer work.

Even if a job is occasional or unpaid, every work experience brings the chance to develop important skills that are valued in the workplace.

A prospective employer looks at your qualities, skills, education, and experience to determine if you would be a good match for a job. At the same time, you need to consider certain factors about the company or the job that are important to you. These factors will help you to focus your job search in areas of work that would be a good match for you. Use the exercise that follows to think about what you want from a career.

What I Want from My Career

Purpose: To identify the elements of a job that are most important to you.

For sections 1 through 10, check all that apply.

1. I prefer to work most with

_____ resources (e.g., environment, money, employees, etc.)
_____ people (e.g., children, peers, the elderly, the poor, etc.)
_____ information (e.g., visuals, numbers, words, etc.)
_____ systems (e.g., social groups, work processes, information systems, etc.)
_____ technology (e.g., computers, cooking equipment, hand tools, machinery, etc.)

2. The types of *resources* I would most enjoy working with are

_____ the environment
_____ money
_____ employees
_____ equipment
_____ other:

3. The types of *people* I would most enjoy working with are

_____ children
_____ peers
_____ the elderly
_____ the poor
_____ other:

4. The types of *information* I would most enjoy working with are

_____ Internet
_____ numbers
_____ visuals
_____ words
_____ other:

5. The types of *systems* I would most enjoy working with are

_____ social groups
_____ work processes
_____ information systems
_____ communication systems
_____ other:

6. The types of *technology* I would most enjoy working with are

_____ computers
_____ cooking equipment
_____ hand tools
_____ machinery
_____ other:

7. The area(s) of the country in which I would like to work is/are

_____ North
_____ Northeast
_____ Southeast
_____ South
_____ Midwest
_____ West
_____ Northwest
_____ Southwest

8. I would like to work in

_____ urban areas
_____ suburban areas
_____ rural areas

9. I would like to work

_____ indoors
_____ outdoors

10. I would like to work in a

_____ casual work environment

_____ formal work environment

11. I would like to work for

_____ a large corporation

_____ a small company

_____ my own business

For sections 12 through 14, complete the statement.

12. The values that are important for me in my work are

_____

_____

_____

_____

13. The amount of job security (e.g., short-term job or long-term job) I need is

_____

_____

_____

_____

14. The amount of salary I want is

_____

_____

_____

_____

Setting a Career Objective

So far you've looked at the employment market and educational requirements for various jobs. You know your qualities, skills, and experiences plus the factors about the company or job that are important to you. Now comes the exciting part—you're ready to combine this research and thinking to come up with one or two occupations for your career objective. Having a career objective will guide your job search and make it easier for you to find a job you will enjoy. Use the following exercise to set your career objective.

YOUR TURN

Where I Am Headed in My Career

Purpose: To identify a career objective. (Note: *The Occupational Outlook Handbook* is an ideal resource for this exercise.)

List all of the occupations that appeal to you.

_____

_____

_____

_____

_____

List the three occupations that are the most interesting to you.

1. _____

2. _____

3. _____

Choose one or two occupations that are the best match for you in terms of your skills or interests.

_____

_____

_____

State the goal you have for your career.

_____

_____

_____

My career objectives are

_____

_____

_____

Components of a Successful Job Search

Having a career objective means you can now plan your job search. Job hunting is hard work, and a successful job search involves a number of tasks.

1. Preparing your resumé
2. Obtaining references/letters of recommendation
3. Finding job openings through
   a. people you know
   b. employers
   c. college placement offices
   d. internships and job shadowing
   e. career fairs
   f. classified ads
   g. private employment agencies
   h. government employment services
   i. job clearinghouses
   j. the Internet

4. Writing cover letters
5. Preparing a portfolio
6. Completing employment applications
7. Interviewing
8. Assessing job offers
9. Declining/accepting offers

Conducting a Successful Job Search

Because job hunting is tough, the first step in launching a successful job search is having the right attitude. You may be lucky enough to find the right job within a few days. Or you may have to hunt for weeks or months before clicking with the best opportunity. A lengthy job search can chip away at your self-belief and self-confidence, especially if you face a lot of rejection and disappointment. Don't let this affect your attitude!

Motivate yourself to keep moving forward. Reward yourself after you send out a round of resumés. Congratulate yourself when an interview appointment comes through for you. Use positive self-talk to reaffirm what you have to offer to prospective employers. Practice visualization. Picture yourself at the job of your dreams, working with colleagues, accomplishing goals, winning praise from the boss. Keeping these images in your mind will help you to overcome the discouragement that is a part of almost every job search.

The next step is planning and organizing your job search. Begin your job search with a plan for tasks 1 through 6 of the process outlined in the previous section. Use the *My Job Search Plan* form to build your plan, highlight the steps of each task, and set goals for the completion of the tasks.

                                                        YOUR TURN

My Job Search Plan

Task:_____

    *Step 1:*_____

    Results needed: _____

    To be accomplished by:_____

Task:_____

    Step 2: _____

    Results needed: _____

    To be accomplished by:_____

Task:_____

    Step 3: _____

    Results needed: _____

    To be accomplished by:_____

Task:_____

    Step 4: _____

    Results needed: _____

    To be accomplished by:_____

Task:_____

    Step 5: _____

    Results needed: _____

    To be accomplished by:_____

Task:_____

    Step 6:   _____

    Results needed: _____

    To be accomplished by:_____

Make photocopies of *My Job Search Plan* and place them either in a three-ring binder or a two-pocket folder. This becomes your job search notebook. Think of this tool as job-search central because it will organize all of the details of your job hunt for easy reference and effective follow-up.

Other forms to include in your job search notebook are the following *My Job Search Notes* and the *Interview Notes* included at the end of this journal. Prepare one page for each company you contact and arrange the pages in your notebook in alphabetical order by company name.

My Job Search Notes

Company: _____

Contact: _____

Contact's title: _____

Address: _____

Telephone: _____

Fax: _____

E-mail: _____

Referred by: _____

Initial contact _____

    Letter or phone? _____ Date: _____

    Result: _____

Follow-up 1

    Letter or phone? _____ Date: _____

    Result: _____

Follow-up 2

    Letter or phone? _____ Date: _____

    Result: _____

Resumé submitted

    ☐ Yes   ☐ No   Date: _____

    Result: _____

First interview

    Date: _____

    Result: _____

    Thank-you note sent: _____

Second interview

    Date: _____

    Result: _____

    Thank-you note sent: _____

Comments:

_____

_____

_____

_____

_____

_____

_____

_____

When your job search is planned and organized, your next step is to research prospective employers offering the kinds of jobs that meet your career objective. Compile a list of companies by consulting the telephone company's Yellow Pages and directories of local chambers of commerce and trade associations, which are available at the library. Then request information about the company from its public relations department, check your public library for business indexes such as *Thomas Register,* or download information from the company's Internet Web site.

TIPS

When researching potential employers, it is important to answer some key questions. For each company that appeals to you, find the answers to the following questions.

> What does the company sell or produce?
> Is the company small or large?
> Is the company a for-profit or not-for-profit enterprise?
> What is the company's reputation in the community and in the industry?
> What are the company's problems?

Record your findings on the following My Prospective Employer Research form and include a form for each company in your job search notebook. Compiling this information will help you formulate questions to ask during your interview.

My Prospective Employer Research

Company: _____

Address: _____

Telephone: _____

Fax: _____

E-mail: _____

This company's recent products, services, or ventures are

_____

_____

_____

This company is   □ Small   □ Large

Number of employees: _____

This company is   □ For-Profit   □ Nonprofit

This company's financial status/earnings profile is _____

_____

_____

_____

This company's reputation in the community is _____

_____

_____

_____

This company's reputation in the industry is

_____

_____

_____

This company's problems are

_____

_____

_____

Comments:

_____

_____

_____

_____

_____

_____

_____

_____

Making It Happen For You!

NANCY LINK, Vice President, Thomson University, ITP

In her position as Vice President, Thomson University at ITP, Nancy Link sees dozens of job candidates coming right out of college and wanting to work for International Thomson Publishing. She has hired straight-A students and those who've pulled Bs and Cs. Grades aren't all that important to Link. Instead, she looks for special qualities in the candidate.

"I look for somebody who's got a personality, who's got passion about something, who has something to give," Link says. "Give me someone who can show me that he or she is going to work hard, that he or she is going to get excited, that the person is going to come to me and ask for guidance.

Link feels an admiration for people who do whatever it takes to land that first job, including working at paid or unpaid internships, going through a temporary placement agency, or taking another job with the company. "This is not only creative, it's also giving you more experience, so why not go for it?" Link says.

"I think if people find a company that they want to work for, they'll do almost any job in order to get into the company. I see that a lot at ITP. They'll do whatever it takes to find a home here. That shows me they'll be committed to the company.

The show of comitment is often enough to get an interview with Link. What does she look for in the candidate at that point? Link looks for someone who asks questions about the business: how the company is structured, who the competitors are, how bright is the company's future, what is the career ladder for the position the person is interested in.

> We have a lot to get done here and I want to hire someone who not only has the skills and abilities to do it, but they've got it in their hearts to get it done too. The head has to balance out with the heart.

"Show me you're interested in the business. That will show me that you have the heart, that you've got that fire in your belly, and it also tells me that you're not going to stick to whatever job duties are in that job description. You're willing to do whatever it takes because you care about the business moving forward, not just what's in it for you.

Once your company research is under way, you next need to hone your networking (see Chapter 4 for a complete discussion of networking) and telephone techniques. Networking involves spreading the word to everyone you know about the job you seek and the qualifications you offer. Start with family and friends, then extend your networking efforts to the managers and executives you meet who can refer you to others in a position to hire.

Networking techniques involve good interpersonal skills—shaking hands, maintaining eye contact, smiling—combined with stating the job title or providing a brief description of your desired position, and letting the person know how you can be reached. Have a supply of business cards printed with your telephone number and e-mail address. On the back of the card print a mini resumé, listing your top skills and attributes. Exchange business cards with people you meet. You never know how your business card will spread the word about your career objective, your skills, and your abilities.

In addition to developing solid networking skills, you'll need to practice effective telephone techniques until they become second nature to you. Stand when you make a phone call. This allows you to project a strong, confident voice. Greet the person who answers the call, state your name, the name of the person you wish to speak to, and the reason for your call. For example,

"Good morning! This is Peter Hess. I'd like to speak with Mr. Anderson please, regarding a job opening." Courtesy and respect for those on the other end of the line will pay dividends as will a smile. True, your smile cannot be seen, but it can be heard because smiling affects your speech quality.

If you feel nervous speaking on the phone, take a few deep breaths before you punch in the number. Visualize the person on the other end of the line smiling when your call comes in and greeting you warmly. If you fear you'll become tongue-tied or forget what you want to say, write out a short script. Practice the script a few times so that you sound natural. You don't want to sound as if you're reciting canned language. (Chapter 5 provides additional tips on using the telephone.)

Networking and telephone techniques will help you get to an interview. What you wear to an interview often means the difference between getting the job or losing your chances. Research shows that a person's appearance is more important to an observer than a person's voice or words. Since you have only ten seconds to make a good first impression, make the most of that initial encounter.

Part of creating that good first impression is the way you dress. Dress standards have changed in the last few years. In many companies, the button-downed look has given way to casual business attire. How will you know what to wear?

One way to determine proper attire for an interview is to go to the prospective employer and park outside the building. Observe the clothing worn by the employees as they enter and leave the building. Be careful not to do this on a holiday or a Friday because many organizations have dress-down policies in effect on these days.

What do you see? People in suits? Women in mix-and-match skirts and blouses? Men in open-necked shirts and casual trousers? Use your observations to decide how button-downed or casual you should go. When in doubt, choose the traditional suit because it's better to be overdressed than underdressed. Whatever you wear, make sure your clothing is clean and pressed to make that first impression a good one.

Developing a Personalized Job Search

Some job seekers leave no stone unturned in their quest for employment. They attack the search with the entire arsenal of strategies from answering classified ads to cold calling prospective employers. Others prefer to focus their efforts, using only three or four different strategies. Develop your own personalized job search by choosing all or some of the following strategies from the job seeker's arsenal.

- ➤ *Network with People You Know.* Many jobs aren't advertised in the Sunday classifieds. Instead they're advertised person to person. To tap into these unadvertised openings, network with people you know. Tell relatives, friends, and colleagues about the type of job you seek and what you can offer a prospective employer. Ask for leads to jobs that might be of interest. Research shows that nearly 50 percent of all successful job seekers found their jobs by networking with people they know.
- ➤ *Cold Call Prospective Employers.* Cold calling is a basic technique used in sales. Since you are "selling" yourself to a prospective employer, cold calling works for job seekers, too. Here's how it works. You choose a prospective employer and arrive unannounced, asking to speak with someone about opportunities in the company. If you promise to take only five minutes of the person's time, you usually can get in. This gives you the chance to make a face-to-face contact and to leave your resumé and portfolio in the event that openings are available. Be aware that cold calling prospective employers is a controversial tactic. Some employers are turned off by this; others are not.
- ➤ *Secure Informational Interviews.* You make an appointment for an informational interview. But instead of applying for a job, you seek information and advice from an industry expert about the field. Informational interviews expand your employer research, multiply your networking contacts, and provide objective feedback from the expert on your qualifications.
- ➤ *Register with College Placement Offices.* Most colleges have job referral services for students and alumni. To tap into this source of job leads, you register by completing an application and including a copy of your resumé, your portfolio, and letters of recommendation. Some referral services match you to employers with openings, while others give you access to a job hotline that you use to match yourself to prospective employers.
- ➤ *Become an Intern/Participate in Job Shadowing.* Participating in an internship is an excellent way to gain real-life experience—and possibly a job— in a career field you are considering. Internships work well for the company, too. Companies often use their intern programs as a source for new hires. Seeing how you work and interact as a team member allows a company to judge your effectiveness and potential as an employee.

Job shadowing is another great way to experience a job firsthand. You spend a few hours or a day following or shadowing someone in your chosen occupation. This gives you a better idea of the ins and outs of a particular job and whether the occupation would be a good match for you.

> *Attend Career Fairs.* Companies send recruiters to career fairs with one goal—to find qualified people for job vacancies. You will have assembled before you a host of potential employers, giving you the opportunity to interview them. Because a career fair is an interview opportunity, the company is looking you over, too, so be sure you dress appropriately for the big day.

Review the list of companies that will be present at the career fair and check all the ones that interest you. Then prioritize the companies you've selected with #1 representing the company that holds the highest interest for you, #2 representing the company that holds the next highest interest for you, and so on. Plan to visit the companies in prioritized order.

Many large career fairs offer maps so you can locate the exhibit areas of the particular companies in which you are interested. Find your target companies on the map and indicate next to the company's name the ranking on your prioritized list. This allows you not only to visualize the stops you'll be making but also to cluster visits if several target companies are located in the same area.

If the first company on your list is swamped with job seekers, move on to the second company on your list. But don't forget to go back to company #1. Cross each company off your list after you've completed your visit.

At each company's exhibit area, introduce yourself to the recruiter and present your business card. Ask questions about the opportunities available at the company, take notes, and be prepared to speak about your accomplishments and goals. Above all, if the company and the job opportunities interest you, be sure to tell the recruiter how you see yourself as a good match for the company. Ask the recruiter if he or she would accept a copy of your resumé right then and there or if the recruiter would prefer that you mail or e-mail the resumé to the company.

> *Answer Classified Ads.* Daily and Sunday local newspapers and professional and trade publications are filled with hundreds of classified ads for jobs. Set up a consistent routine of checking these periodicals. Respond promptly to any ad that attracts you, and keep a record of every ad you answer.

- ➤ *Register with Private Employment Agencies.* Private employment agencies can offer temporary jobs, permanent jobs in general fields, temporary or permanent jobs in specialized areas, or executive-level positions. Registering with a private employment agency requires completing an application. Getting a job through a private employment agency requires either the employer or you to pay a fee for the service. Fees are usually a percentage of your first year's salary. Ask whether the employer or you will pay the fee and understand the financial arrangements before you use a private employment agency to find a job.
- ➤ *Access Government Employment Services.* Most states have a job service that offers free referrals to local and statewide jobs. Check with your state's Department of Labor for information about these referrals. Look in the phone book for the number of the Department of Labor, visit the agency Web site, or check with your local library. Some libraries have a job service computer database that you can use.
- ➤ *Register with Job Clearinghouses.* Federal, private, and specialized job clearinghouses collect and distribute employment information such as job openings posted by employers and job qualifications posted by job seekers. Check with your local library for information about registering with national and statewide job clearinghouses.
- ➤ *Tap into Internet Resources.* More than 11,000 Web sites post job openings, including corporate Web sites, college placement offices with on-line capability, local newspapers that publish an electronic version of the paper, and state and federal employment agencies that maintain job databases. You can also use the Internet to establish a personal home page. But keep in mind that not every employer uses the Internet. Tapping into Internet resources should not be your only job-hunting strategy.

Focus your personalized job search by completing the following exercise.

My Personalized Job Search Plan

Purpose: To identify strategies you will use in your job search.

The strategies I will use for my job search are (check all that apply)

_____ networking with people I know
_____ cold calling prospective employers
_____ securing informational interviews
_____ registering with college placement offices
_____ becoming an intern
_____ participating in job shadowing
_____ attending career fairs
_____ answering classified ads
_____ registering with private employment agencies
_____ accessing government employment services
_____ registering with job clearinghouses
_____ tapping into Internet resources

Prioritize the strategies you just identified. Place a 1 before the strategy that is most effective for your circumstances, a 2 before the strategy that is the next most effective, and so on.

My top five job search strategies are:

1. _____

2. _____

3. _____

4. _____

5. _____

Complete a My Job Search Plan form for each of your top five strategies.

Place these forms in your job search notebook.

Writing Your Resumé

Your resumé is a snapshot of your experience and qualifications. Most resumés usually contain the following:

> ➤ your name, address, telephone number, and e-mail address.
> ➤ your career objective (optional).
> ➤ summary of your qualifications.
> ➤ your education (i.e., names and locations of schools attended, dates of attendance, type of program, diploma or degree received).
> ➤ your work experience, including internships and community volunteer positions. Include the job title, name and location of the employer, and dates of employment.
> ➤ professional licenses.
> ➤ your military experience (i.e., branch, length of service, major responsibilities, special training).
> ➤ your membership in organizations.
> ➤ any special skills, honors, awards, or achievements.
> ➤ information about the availability of references.

Because presenting a career objective is optional, you'll need to think carefully about whether to include one.

Maybe your objective states: "Entry-level sales position with the potential for growth and advancement" or "Senior-level management position with money management responsibility." Wanting a job that offers growth and advancement is almost a given. This doesn't tell the human resource director anything new. Likewise, most senior-level positions include money management responsibilities. If the company to which you've applied has current openings only in public relations or marketing, your resumé will go in the No pile.

You can arrange the information on your resumé in one of three popular formats:

1. chronological format
2. functional format
3. combination format

The chronological format (see page 59) lists your most recent job first, and then your other jobs in reverse chronological order. This is the most common format for a resumé.

The functional format (see page 60) transforms your work experience into functions and skills. If you are a career changer or someone with little or no formal work experience, this is an ideal format for you.

The combination format (see page 61) lists your functions and skills and shows your job history in reverse chronological order.

Use the following data sheet to compile the information you will use in your resumé.

YOUR TURN

Data Sheet for My Resumé

Name: _____

Address: _____

Telephone Number: _____ E-mail: _____

Career Objective: _____

_____

My Qualifications: _____

_____

Education

College or Other Postsecondary School #1: _____

Address: _____

Date Started: _____ Date Ended: _____

Years Completed or Degree Received: _____ Course of Study: _____

Courses Relevant to Career Objective:_____

_____

Honors:_____

_____

Extracurricular Activities:_____

_____

College or Other Postsecondary School #2: _____

Address: _____

Date Started: _____ Date Ended: _____

Years Completed or Degree Received: _____ Course of Study: _____

Courses Relevant to Career Objective:_____

_____

Honors:_____

_____

Extracurricular Activities:_____

_____

High School

Address: _____

Date Started: _____ Date Ended: _____

Years Completed or Degree Received: _____ Course of Study: _____

Courses Relevant to Career Objective: _____

_____

Honors:_____

_____

Extracurricular Activities:_____

_____

Work Experience

Job Title: _____

Employer's Name and Address: _____

Supervisor's Name: _____

Date Started: _____ Date Ended: _____

Description of Responsibilities and Skills Used: _____

_____

_____

_____

_____

Job Title: _____

Employer's Name and Address: _____

Supervisor's Name: _____

Date Started: _____ Date Ended: _____

Description of Responsibilities and Skills Used: _____

_____

_____

_____

_____

Job Title: _____

Employer's Name and Address: _____

Supervisor's Name: _____

Date Started: _____ Date Ended: _____

Description of Responsibilities and Skills Used: _____

_____

_____

_____

_____

Professional Licenses

Name/Number of License: _____

Licensing Agency: _____

Military Experience

Rank: _____ Branch of Service: _____

Date Started: _____ Date Ended: _____

Description of Responsibilities and Skills Used: _____

_____

_____

_____

_____

Date Started: _____ Date Ended: _____

Description of Responsibilities and Skills Used: _____

_____

_____

_____

_____

Special Training: _____

_____

Personal Data

Awards, Honors, and Special Achievements: _____

_____

_____

Hobbies and Special Interests: _____

_____

_____

Foreign Languages: _____

_____

_____

Organizations and Offices Held: _____

_____

_____

Volunteer Work: _____

_____

_____

References

Education/Employer Reference: _____

Name and Title: _____

Address: _____

Phone: _____

Education/Employer Reference: _____

Name and Title: _____

Address: _____

Phone: _____

Character Reference: _____

Name and Title: _____

Address: _____

Phone: _____

Resumé Sample: Chronological Format

Jesse Smith
23 First Street • Albany, NY 12208
(518) 555-3647 • jsmith@aol.com

WORK EXPERIENCE:

September 1992 to Present	Assistant Bookkeeper, Achievement Office Sales/Service, Albany, NY. Aid in bookkeeping, payroll services, and tax preparation.
September 1993 to May 1994	Internship at Goldworthy & Ames Certified Public Accountants, Albany, NY. Provided tax preparation assistance for five major clients.
September 1991 to April 1992	Tutor, Teaching and Learning Center, The College of Saint Rose, Albany, NY. Provided tutoring assistance in Math 121, 122 and Statistics I and II to students on an individual basis.
May 1990 to September 1994	Groundskeeper. Albany High School, Albany, NY. Maintained school grounds during summer break.

EDUCATION:

September 1990 to May 1994	The College of Saint Rose, Albany, NY. Bachelor of Science degree in Business Administration conferred in May 1994 Accounting GPA: 3.8 Overall GPA: 3.5

COMPUTER SKILLS:

Excel, Lotus 1-2-3, WordPerfect, Microsoft Word, IBM and Apple applications

LEADERSHIP EXPERIENCES:

Supervisor and team leader of client audits
Co-captain 1989–1990 State Championship basketball team
Two gold medals and one bronze—Team Handball—
Empire State Games

REFERENCES:

Available upon request.

Resumé Sample: Functional Format

Jesse Smith
23 First Street • Albany, NY 12208
(518) 555-3647 • jsmith@aol.com

SKILLS / ACHIEVEMENTS:	Supervisor and team leader of client audits.
	Excellent computer skills, including Excel, Lotus 1-2-3, WordPerfect, Microsoft Word, IBM and Apple applications.
	Working with clients and interpreting their needs.
	Working under the pressure of deadlines.
EMPLOYMENT HISTORY:	Assistant Bookkeeper, Achievement Office Sales/Service, Albany, NY. 1992 to present.
	Intern, Goldworthy & Ames Certified Public Accountants, Albany, NY. 1993 to 1994.
	Tutor, Teaching and Learning Center, The College of Saint Rose, Albany, NY. 1991 to 1992.
	Groundskeeper, Albany High School, Albany, NY. 1990 to 1994.
EDUCATION:	Bachelor of Science degree, Business Administration, The College of Saint Rose, Albany, NY, May 1994.
RELEVANT COURSES:	Financial Accounting, Behavioral Science in Business, Urban Economics, Managerial Economics, Financial Information Systems, Taxation, Strategic Marketing Planning, Investment Theory, New Business Ventures and the Entrepreneur, Performance and Financial Auditing
REFERENCES:	Available upon request.

Resumé Sample: Combination Format

Jesse Smith
23 First Street • Albany, NY 12208
(518) 555-3647 • jsmith@aol.com

SKILLS /   Supervisor and team leader of client audits.
ACHIEVEMENTS: Excellent computer skills, including Excel, Lotus 1-2-3,
WordPerfect, Microsoft Word, IBM and Apple applications.
Working with clients and interpreting their needs.
Working under the pressure of deadlines.

WORK EXPERIENCE:

September 1992 to Present	Assistant Bookkeeper, Achievement Office Sales/Service, Albany, NY. Aid in bookkeeping, payroll services, and tax preparation.
September 1993 to May 1994	Internship at Goldworthy & Ames Certified Public Accountants, Albany, NY. Provided tax preparation assistance for five major clients.
September 1991 to April 1992	Tutor, Teaching and Learning Center, The College of Saint Rose, Albany, NY. Provided tutoring assistance in Math 121, 122 and Statistics I and II to students on an individual basis.
May 1990 to September 1994	Groundskeeper. Albany High School, Albany, NY. Maintained school grounds during summer break.

EDUCATION:

September 1990 to May 1994	The College of Saint Rose, Albany, NY Bachelor of Science degree in Business Administration conferred in May 1994 Accounting GPA: 3.8 Overall GPA: 3.5

REFERENCES: Available upon request.

Resumé Requirements

No matter which format you choose, keep your resumé to one page, unless you have extensive work experience to cite. Another exception to this rule may be if you are applying for positions within the education field, in which resume length is less strict. Prepare your resumé on white or ivory bond paper with at least one-inch margins all around.

Describe your skills and abilities in short phrases instead of full sentences and use action words to describe your accomplishments. Avoid using humor, which almost always falls flat, and be truthful in everything you list on the resumé.

Have the content well organized, make sure your resumé looks neat, and that it's free of grammar and spelling errors. Don't trust your word processor's grammar- and spell-check programs to find your mistakes! Eyeball the resumé yourself or better yet ask someone with experience to edit and proof the resumé for you.

Obtaining References and Letters of Recommendation

As you create your resumé, think about people who would be willing to vouch for you as a reference or who would be willing to write a letter of recommendation. Select three or four people who know you well and who can comment positively about your work habits, skills, and personal qualities. Instructors, coaches, and job supervisors are good choices because they can be objective. Relatives and friends aren't good choices for obvious reasons. Nobody ever got a job because of praise from his or her mother.

Ask your potential references if they feel they could write a strong recommendation. Choose only those who can provide this for you. To make the task easier for your references, provide a copy of your resumé or other information about your direction and background.

The people you choose as references should be available by telephone when a prospective employer calls. If a person isn't easily available by telephone, ask the person to provide a letter of recommendation. A letter of recommendation offers a written appraisal of your work habits, skills, and personal qualities. Ask the person to address the letter To Whom It May Concern so that you can use the letter over and over again.

Phone references are becoming the norm with many companies. Be careful, as I have seen numerous situations in which people believe that they have a positive reference, only to find out the opposite. Ask a potential reference a very specific question such as: Would you be willing to serve as a *positive* reference for me in my search for a new position? Most people will not say yes to that question unless they truly intend to represent you in a positive light. If the person is not able to say yes to this question, ask them why. ■

Writing Cover Letters

When you answer a classified job ad or another job listing, you send a copy of your resumé along with a one-page cover letter. Your cover letter shows your particular interest in a specific job, highlights your experience or skills, and gets the employer to read your resumé and to call you for an interview.

Cover letters must be individually tailored to each job posting you respond to. Here's a formula for can-do cover letters:

> ➤ Address your cover letter to a specific person, if possible. Make sure you spell the person's name correctly.
> ➤ Use the first paragraph to indicate the purpose of the letter. Note the job you are applying for and where you learned about the opening. If you were referred to the company, mention the name of the person who made the referral.
> ➤ Use the second paragraph to show why and how your skills and experience would be assets to the company.
> ➤ Use the third paragraph to ask for an interview and to tell the employer how you can be reached.

Since your cover letter will contribute to the employer's first impression of you, use a positive, upbeat tone and be certain that the cover letter is like the resumé—well-organized, neat, and free from errors. A sample cover letter follows.

Jesse Smith
23 First Street • Albany, NY 12208
(518) 555-3647 • jsmith@aol.com

January 15, 1999

Ms. Amee Wong
Human Resources Manager
Cutler & Quigley, Inc.
35 South Hills Road
Clifton Park, NY 12065

Dear Ms. Wong:

I am applying for the position of assistant accountant that was advertised in the January 14, 1999 edition of the Albany *Times Union*. My resumé is enclosed.

I am currently employed as an assistant bookkeeper at Achievement Office Sales/Service in Albany where I aid in bookkeeping, payroll services, and tax preparation. I have excellent computer skills and interact well with clients. I believe that my skills, experience, and motivation will benefit Cutler & Quigley, Inc.

I will be happy to make an appointment for an interview. You can reach me at 555-3647. I will plan to call you on January 23 to answer any questions you may have.

Sincerely,
Jesse Smith

enclosure

Preparing a Portfolio

While your cover letter and resumé get your foot in the door, a portfolio often clinches the deal. A portfolio is a collection of documents showing proof of your accomplishments, performance, and work history. You can include some or all of the following:

> an unofficial copy of your college transcript, showing your courses, number of credits, and letter grades.
> a list of courses you are currently taking.

- certificates of achievement that you received for volunteering in the community, attaining the dean's list, for completing a self-improvement workshop or for courses you've taken in Microsoft Word, Excel, Access, or PowerPoint.
- letters of recommendation.
- projects you completed at work or during your educational experiences that showcase your highest skill level. You could include written papers from a course in which you excelled, brochures you created at work, copies of your action plans showing proof that you've implemented the various steps.

Package these materials in a colorful, two-pocket folder. Don't enclose your originals; make photocopies of all materials. After all, the employer may be so impressed with your portfolio that he or she decides to keep it. Place one of your business cards in the portfolio (many two-pocket folders have die-cut slots designed to hold business cards) for a crisp, professional presentation.

Practice showing your portfolio. With a friend acting as a prospective employer, remove each item from the portfolio and explain its significance. Have your friend evaluate how well you showcased your materials and make any suggestions for improving your presentation.

PITFALLS

Creating a portfolio is an exercise in self-discovery and can be quite exciting. Be careful, however, that you do not fill your portfolio with materials that really do not relate to you gaining meaningful employment. Make sure that your materials are relevant, timely, and help the employer to understand why you are the ideal person to hire.

Completing Employment Applications

Some employers may ask you to fill out an employment application before you are interviewed. You'll notice that the form asks for most of the information contained in your resume. The application arranges the information for the employer's convenience.

To make the task of completing employment applications easier, bring a copy of your resumé with you. Follow the directions on the application carefully. Most will ask you to print or type the information. Do so neatly without spelling or grammar errors. For any section that doesn't apply to you, write NA—which means not applicable—in the space. This tells the employer that you didn't skip over that section by mistake. You don't have to provide any information that is discriminatory, including your age, race, religion, marital status, and arrest record.

Launching Your Job Search

You've prepared your action plan—My Job Search Plan— organized your research and contacts in your job search notebook. As you move through the steps of your job search, take time periodically to carefully and objectively evaluate your progress. If you're not receiving offers, you may have to change your approach.

Attaining and Maintaining a Positive Attitude

Attaining and maintaining a positive attitude throughout your job search may be the toughest task of all. One excellent strategy for stopping anxiety or depression from chipping away at your positive attitude is forming a job search team.

A job search team is a support group of other job seekers who are all looking for different jobs. Pull together five to ten job hunters and agree to meet every week. The meetings should be designed to encourage and support each other, to share job leads and job-hunting advice, and to exchange learning experiences and interviewing tips.

Have each person set goals for the week ahead—"I will mail resumés to ten companies this week," "I will spend an hour a day researching jobs on the Internet"—and then report to the group at the next meeting on his or her accomplishments. After two weeks, ask each person to complete the following exercise.

Five Positive Results I've Realized from My Job Search Team

Purpose: To evaluate the positive results of meeting with your job search team.

1. _____

2. _____

3. _____

4. _____

5. _____

ELEMENTS OF EXCELLENCE

As you come to the end of this chapter, reflect on the next step of your journey of a thousand miles.

- ➤ You matched yourself to a career; set a career objective.
- ➤ You learned the components of and how to conduct a successful, personalized job search.
- ➤ You discovered how to create a resumé, cover letter, and portfolio.
- ➤ You picked up tips on attaining and maintaining a positive attitude.

You're on a roll, so don't quit now. Step into Chapter 3 where you'll focus on success before, during, and after the interview. Come on, let's go! ■

Read All About It!

Anderson, Walter. *The Confidence Course: Seven Steps to Self-fulfillment.* New York: HarperPerennial, 1998.

Boles, Richard Nelson. *What Color Is Your Parachute? A Practical Manual for Job Hunters and Career-Changers.* Berkeley, CA: Ten Speed Press, 1998.

Dimitrius, Jo-Ellan, Ph.D., & Mark Mazzarella. *Reading People: How to Understand People and Predict Their Behavior Any Time, Any Place.* New York: Random House, 1998.

Josefowitz, Natasha. *Paths to Power: A Woman's Guide from First Job to Top Executive.* Reading, MA: Addison-Wesley, 1990.

Kaplan, Burton. *Winning People Over: 14 Days to Power and Confidence.* Upper Saddle River, NJ: Prentice Hall, 1996.

Moreau, Daniel. *Take Charge of Your Career: Survive and Profit from a Mid-Career Change.* Washington, DC: Kiplinger Books, 1996.

Richardson, Bradley G. *JobSmarts for Twentysomethings.* New York: Vintage Books, 1995.

Rosenberg, Howard. *How to Succeed without a Career Path: Jobs for People with No Corporate Ladder.* Manassas Park, VA: Impact Publications, 1995.

Scott, Steven K. *Simple Steps to Impossible Dreams: The Fifteen Power Secrets of the World's Most Successful People.* New York: Simon & Schuster, 1998.

Tieger, Paul D., & Barbara Barron-Tieger. *The Art of Speed Reading People: Harness the Power of Personality Type and Create What You Want in Business and in Life.* New York: Little Brown, 1998.

Books I've Read

Use the space provided to list the books you've read in this subject area and to reflect on what you've learned from reading them.

1._____

2._____

3._____

4._____

5._____

Internet Resources

http://www.selfgrowth.com

Self-Improvement Online, Inc. This Web site contains information on personal growth and provides links to other sites and newsgroups.

http://stats.bls.gov

U.S. Department of Labor's Bureau of Labor Statistics posts the *Occupational Outlook Handbook,* containing the latest job trend information.

http://www.ajb.dni.us/

America's Job Bank contains job listings posted by the public Employment Service and links to your state's employment office.

My Favorite Internet Sites

Use the space provided to list your favorite Internet sites.

1. _____

2. _____

3. _____

4. _____

5. _____

Chapter *3*
>>>>>>>

Success Before, During, and After the Interview

Seeing things from the interviewer's angle as well as your own is at the heart of a successful job interview. But attaining a successful job interview begins even before you walk into the office of a prospective employer. You must research both the company and the job, know how to put your best foot forward during the interview, handle typical and tough questions, and know how to accept or decline a job offer based on whether the offer represents the right relationship. This chapter will help you to achieve success before, during, and after the interview.

After completing this chapter, you should understand

> If there is any one secret of success, it lies in the ability to get the other person's point of view and see things from his angle as well as from your own.

HENRY FORD,
AMERICAN
AUTOMOBILE
PIONEER

> the various types of interviews you may face.
> how to prepare for an interview.
> what interviewers look for in a candidate.
> how interviewers treat candidates.
> how to shine during an interview.
> what to do after an interview.
> how to assess whether a job offer is right for you.

If your cover letter and resume have done their job, you'll be contacted to schedule an interview. The interview is the prospective employer's opportunity to evaluate your personal qualities, skills, and experience, but it is also your chance to learn as much as you can about the company and about the job. Since everything rides on

< **70** >

how you behave before, during, and after the interview, preparation is vital. Making a good impression, asking intelligent questions, and showing your professionalism and interest are success signposts along your journey of a thousand miles.

Types of Interviews

What will your interview be like? Your interview may last only 15 minutes or may stretch for an hour or longer. The interview might be conducted over the telephone with just you and the personnel manager, or the interview might take place as a conference call with you and a search committee. Telephone interviews save the employer time and money, especially if you are interviewing for a job located at a distance from where you live. However, most interviews are done in person. In-person interviews can be conducted one-on-one with the hiring manager or done with a search committee.

An in-person interview gives you a chance to see the actual work location and to meet some of the people you might be working with. Of course, having you on their turf gives the employer and your potential colleagues a chance to look you over as well. That thought combined with the importance of the interview will probably make you nervous. You know that this is your big chance to impress someone who can offer you a job, and you don't want to lose the opportunity. If you take the time before the interview to prepare and get psyched, chances are good that you will have a successful interview.

Preparing for the Interview

Part of your preparation for the interview is researching both the company and the job. Chapter 2 contains strategies for doing initial research on the company. By contacting the company's public relations department, accessing business indexes at your library, or logging onto the company's Internet Web site, you should be able to find information about what the company sells or produces, if the company is small or large, if the company is for-profit or not-for-profit, what the company's reputation is in both the community and in the industry, and the kinds of problems the company might be facing. Review the form on which you captured this information—My Prospective Employer

Research—which is stored in your job search notebook. With this basic information, you can now begin more in-depth research about the company.

Obtain copies of the company's mission statement and annual reports. When you are contacted about scheduling an interview, ask the person who calls to send you a copy of the company's mission statement and annual report for the current year and the previous year. If the current year's annual report isn't prepared yet, ask for the reports from the last two years. When you receive these materials, read them carefully, making notes about the company's significant achievements as well as their challenges. Then think about and list what you can do for the company.

Determine if you know anyone associated with the company. Scan the list of senior staff or the members of the board of directors. Do any of the names ring a bell with you? Run the names by your job search team. Do any of the members know anyone associated with the company? Check with your family, colleagues, and your friends to see if anyone has a link to anyone connected to the company.

If you are able to uncover a connection to someone within the company or on the board, telephone that individual explaining that you have a job interview scheduled and that you're interested in learning more about the company. Most people you call will be glad to take ten minutes to give you an insider's view.

Try to focus the discussion around the challenges the company currently faces, remembering that opportunities are often disguised as problems. Ask also if your contact has any information about the job for which you will be interviewing or if the person knows of anyone inside the company who would be willing to speak with you about the job.

Scan databases of local business periodicals. Head to your local library's magazine and newspaper section and ask the librarian to point you in the direction of database indexes for local business periodicals. Do a search by company name for articles about the company that have appeared in the last six months. From the hits you get, read the full text articles and add notes about the company to your job search notebook.

Read current and back issues of the daily newspaper. While you are in the periodicals section, ask the librarian for a cumulative index for the daily newspaper. Some indexes may be bound into books, whereas others may be computer-based. Do a keyword search by the name of the company and read a selection of articles about the company that have appeared within the last year. Make notes about your findings and add them to your job search notebook. Once you've completed your in-depth research about the company, start researching information about the job itself. Chapter 2 recommended that you check the *Occupational Outlook Handbook* for a general description of your desired job. It's a good place to start, but keep in mind that job titles and descriptions may vary among different employers. You'll want to find out as much information as possible about the specific job for which you will be interviewing. Here's how to do that:

1. *Obtain a copy of the job description.* When you are called about scheduling an interview, ask the person from the company to send you a copy of the job description. Review the duties and responsibilities and assess how closely you come to being a match for the position. Note also if the job description contains a salary range.

2. *Check salary ranges for jobs. Occupational Outlook Handbook* and *National Survey of Professional, Administrative, Technical, and Clerical Pay* contain salary ranges for various jobs. Try to match the job title or job description to the listing in these library reference books to compare the salary range offered by the company to the typical salary range for that job.

3. *Speak with your company contact.* Your company contact may know something about the job and may be willing to share this information with you. But keep in mind that if your contact happens to be a member of the search committee charged with filling the position, he or she may feel that speaking to you about the job outside the context of an interview could be viewed as a conflict of interest. Respect this and withdraw your request, but ask if your contact can recommend anyone else you could talk to.

4. *Check among the people in your network or on your job search team.* Find out if anyone you know is connected to someone working in a similar job. You might ask if someone in your network knows anyone who works or has worked for the company. Speaking with someone already working in a similar job or someone with present or past ties to the company can provide you with an invaluable insider's viewpoint.

After you've researched the company and the job, you should start to feel more comfortable because you've turned a huge unknown—what the company is about and what the job requires—into solid information. You can now use that information to gain more self-confidence by role-playing the interview.

Role-playing is, simply, acting. You pretend to be a job seeker and a partner pretends to be a prospective employer. You both act out the interview, and then you and your partner evaluate your performance. Role-playing gives you the chance to practice answering interview questions so you will be prepared when the real interview takes place. Think of role-playing as the rehearsal that comes before the actual performance. Actors and actresses wouldn't dream of stepping out on a stage without having practiced their lines. Likewise, you shouldn't think of entering a real interview without having logged in some rehearsal time. You'll have a chance to practice role-playing later in this chapter.

Another important factor to consider in preparing for your interview is your appearance. Chapter 2 discussed creating a good first impression in the way you dress. You'll want to stick to the basics, which is usually a clean, conservative, well-pressed suit. This applies to both men and women. Don't go to extremes with skimpy clothes, wild colors, large jewelry, massive body piercings, too much makeup, sunglasses, or sneakers. Avoid perfumes or aftershave. Your appearance is determined not only by the clothing you choose but how you conduct yourself during the interview. Here are some suggestions for you to consider before the interview to make sure that your behavior shows your professionalism.

> *Know the exact location of the interview and the best route to get there.* Arrive for the interview ten minutes early. It looks bad if you are late, and you will be frazzled by the time you get there. If you get there early, you have the chance to visit the restroom to freshen up—comb your hair, pop in a breath mint, and straighten your clothing. If you feel nervous and if you're worried about offering the interviewer a cold, clammy handshake, here's a secret. Run your hands under hot water until your hands feel really warm. Dry them thoroughly with a paper towel and rub them hard. This will keep your hands warm and dry until you walk confidently into the office and offer your hand in greeting.

> *Bring a copy of your portfolio plus two or three copies of your resume.* Make sure that the portfolio is a copy the interviewer may keep, not your original. If the interviewer has misplaced the resume you sent, you can provide a backup copy. The interviewer may want you to meet other people in the company but may not think about or have time to make photocopies of your resume. That's a problem. Having extras with you will show that you are a problem solver.

> *Pack a briefcase.* Include a pen, a small notebook, your list of references, a list of questions you have for the interviewer, and your planning calendar. You may be required to complete an employment application, and you may wish to make notes during the interview. The interviewer may ask for your list of references. If the interviewer wants you to

return for a follow-up interview, you can set the date in your planning calendar.

> *Avoid eating, chewing gum, or smoking* in the reception area or in the interview room.

> *Be courteous to all you meet.* Smile, remember to say "please" and "thank you," and don't interrupt someone who is speaking.

> *Make sure you know the interviewer's name.* Present your business card and ask for the interviewer's card. This way you'll know the person's name and you'll have the interviewer's title and the company's mailing address for the follow-up letter that you will send after the interview.

> *During the interview, don't criticize or complain* about former employers, discuss your financial or personal problems, or get into arguments about controversial topics such as politics or religion.

> *Be ready to take more than one test.* The interviewer may ask you to take a skills or aptitude test, a medical examination, or a drug test.

> *Don't bring up the subject of salary and benefits.* You need to learn specifics about the job first before you can judge whether the salary and benefits are attractive. Your asking about money right off the bat gives the interviewer the impression that money is all you care about. The job that you can do is of paramount importance to the company, so you want to give the impression that the job is of paramount importance to you, too.

Think of it this way. Preparing for an interview is just the same as getting ready for a final exam. By being fully prepared, you will feel more comfortable and confident, and you'll ace any interview.

Making It Happen For You!

CONNIE DAVIS, The Arc of the United States

"The resume has to do a good sales job for the applicant in order to be considered for an interview," according to Connie Davis, Director of Business Services for The Arc of the United States in Arlington, Texas. "I look for education, job longevity, job description matches, grammar, and spelling."

If the sales pitch is a good one, Davis invites candidates to interviews. She conducts a standard interview, discussing both the mission of the not-for-profit agency and the position.

"The one question I almost always ask is: 'I've told you about the requirements of the position, how do you feel your qualifications meet our needs?' The answer to this question tells me if the applicant has listened to the job description, how much job experience he or she has in this area, and what ideas he or she has in applying this experience or ability. It also helps me to determine the applicant's ability to think under pressure."

> In most cases, this [the resumé] is the first contact that an applicant has with the company.

What makes a bad interview? "No eye contact," Davis says. "Also when a candidate talks around questions without answering them. If the question is asked, it deserves a direct answer."

For those preparing for interviews with her organization, Davis offers the following advice. "Learn something about the organization. If this is a first job, have someone help you by practicing. Be prepared to talk about your qualifications and work experience. Dress properly for the interview—conservative, not flashy. Be prompt."

What Interviewers Look for in a Candidate

An interviewer always represents the interests of the company, and the interviewer's challenge is to find the right person to fill a given position. You have your own interests in mind, and your challenge during the interview is to convince the interviewer that you are the right person for the position. In other words, you have to "sell" the idea that you are the best person for the job. Interviewers also look for a candidate who is enthusiastic. Have an upbeat tone to your voice. Visualize yourself accepting the job offer and working at the company and let the excitement from that image be reflected in your speech, your body language, and your gestures.

Interviewers also look for a candidate who is committed to excellence, to teamwork, to professional growth, and to development. If you can demonstrate examples from past jobs, your education, or your personal life that show that you share those same commitments, it will add to the success of your job interview.

Interviewing means that you have to perform. Your performance should be based on who you really are as a person. Remember your values, beliefs, and identity as you answer questions. Do not put on a show in hopes of giving the employer an inflated image of who you really are. The best thing you can do in an interview is be prepared . . . and be your self. ■

How Interviewers Treat Candidates

Most interviewers want you to do your best, but how they treat you during the interview may not be designed with that in mind. Although many interviewers will be gracious, you may encounter others who are gruff, argumentative, and downright nasty. Is this an act? It could be! The interviewer may be testing you to see how you react under pressure and stress. Make sure you pass this test by being respectful and polite at all times. Don't lose your temper, even when provoked. Maintain your cool.

One way an interviewer may try to rattle you is by asking sensitive or personal questions. Questions relating to race, gender, age, religion, and marital status are discriminatory and sometimes illegal, but some interviewers ask them anyway. So what should you do? Replying "That's none of your business" is the truthful answer, but it won't get you anywhere, and, in fact, may even antagonize the interviewer. Your best bet is to answer in a way that gets the interview back on track while sparing the interviewer any embarrassment (after all, some interviewers may not realize that some questions are inappropriate).

For example, the interviewer may ask your age. If you don't mind answering, tell how old you are, but keep in mind that you are not obligated to reply to such a question. If you're uncomfortable answering, phrase your reply this way: "The ad for this position didn't indicate a concern about age. I believe the ad focused on computer skills. I'd like to demonstrate my abilities with WordPerfect."

If your interview is filled with questions that seem to focus on inappropriate subject areas, the interviewer may be testing you, trying to make you lose your cool. Don't let this happen! Often the interviewer will praise you for maintaining control, and that will be your clue that it was all a test. On the other hand, if the interviewer persists in hammering you with questions that are discriminatory and doesn't let you know that it was a test, maybe it wasn't. That may indicate that you would be better off not working for that company.

How to Put Your Best Foot Forward in an Interview

By being prepared, you'll be able to put your best foot forward during your interview. Use these suggestions to make sure that you shine:

Use engaged posture and body language. When you are invited into the interview room, introduce yourself to the interviewer, smile, and shake hands with a firm but not bone-crushing grip. This brief window of time will make or break the interview for you, according to psychologists.

Researchers who have analyzed job interviews believe that most interviewers make up their minds about job candidates within the first 30 seconds of meeting them. This decision is based on what psychologists call the halo effect, meaning the effect meeting you for the first time has on the interviewer. If you trip on the carpet as you enter the office, the person meeting you for the first time will think you're clumsy. If you enter the office smiling and exuding self-confidence, the person meeting you for the first time will think you're self-assured, so make the most of the halo effect.

Don't sit down until the interviewer invites you to take a seat and then directs you to a chair. Place your briefcase on the floor or on a chair next to you. Don't place any of your belongings on the interviewer's desk.

After you are asked to be seated, sit up straight and focus on the interviewer. Pretend that you want to make a friend of this person. Maintain eye contact, lean forward a little, and keep your arms open, not crossed. Your body language speaks louder than your words. If you lean back in your chair with arms crossed, you tell the interviewer that you either lack confidence or that you don't care about the job, the company, or the interviewer. Let your posture and body language show that you are sincere, interested, and enthusiastic.

Listen actively. The Greek philosopher Zeno wrote: "We have two ears and one mouth that we may listen the more and talk the less." Some people listen with only one ear. That means they take in only enough of the conversation to be able to smile and nod at the speaker and throw in an occasional "Uh-huh" to keep the speaker happy and the conversation rolling. That's passive listening. Active listening means that you listen with both ears: You concentrate on the speaker, you participate in the conversation, and your mind focuses on both.

To help you listen actively be physically prepared to hear. Sit close to the speaker so you can hear well, ask that doors and windows be closed to block out noise and distractions, and watch the speaker's nonverbal cues, which will help you interpret the message.

After you are physically prepared to hear, you must be open to listening. That means you must be willing to receive the speaker's message in a non-judgmental way. This is hard because in most conversations, people tend to focus on the contradictions and errors of the message while the speaker is talking. Being open to listening requires you to accept willingly the speaker's right to say the message, to let the message enter your consciousness, and to evaluate the message once you've understood it. Listening in this way communicates to the speaker that you believe he or she is important and that the speaker's ideas have value. In return, the speaker will be more open to you and will feel less defensive because he or she will know that you are not only listening but hearing what is being said.

Being an open listener also means you are curious about other people. If you can allow your curiosity to overcome your need to judge the speaker and to defend your own position, your efforts will be rewarded. You'll find that you'll learn much more than you thought you could.

Asking questions will satisfy your curiosity and allow you to clarify your understanding of the speaker's message. The best questions to ask are open-ended questions that begin with "what," "how," and "why." Questions such as "What is the mission statement of the company?" "How does the company feel about professional development activities for new hires?" and "Why did the last person who held this job leave the position?" require the speaker to respond with an explanation and are designed to get more detail.

Close-ended questions—those that can be answered with yes or no—limit the exchange of information. But these questions can be helpful if you want to be clear about your understanding of the speaker's message. For example: "Did you say that the training period is six weeks long?"

Answer questions concisely and honestly. Some interviewers will ask you specific, targeted questions; others will say simply, "What can you tell me about yourself?" Think before you reply, ask for clarification of anything you don't understand about the question, and follow the interviewer's lead in answering. For specific, targeted questions, give a brief, to-the-point response. For open-ended questions, you can speak at length but try to be concise and avoid rambling or getting off the subject.

No matter what questions you are asked, answer them honestly. Don't give a reply you think the interviewer wants to hear and don't lie. If you do, you may find that your dishonesty comes back to haunt you later.

Be ready to ask questions. Your initial and in-depth research about the company and the job combined with the information you gain from your conversation with the interviewer should make it easy for you to think of questions to ask. As questions occur to you, jot them in your notebook and be sure you ask them at an appropriate moment.

If the interviewer has covered all of your questions during the conversation, you may encounter that awkward moment when he or she asks you "What questions do you have?" You could mumble something like "Well, you've already covered everything," but interviewers expect you to ask questions. Don't panic! Interviewers plan their questions in advance, so there's no reason why you shouldn't have questions prepared ahead of time that you can ask during any interview. Here are some questions for you to consider. Write them on the last page of your small notebook, so you can turn to them immediately and avoid an uncomfortable silence.

> What is this company like as a place to work?
> What can you tell me about the culture and company's values?
> What are the challenges your company is facing?
> Could you tell me about the primary people I would be working with?
> What career opportunities exist beyond the entry-level position?
> What do you consider ideal experience for this job?
> The job sounds really exciting—what are the drawbacks?
> How will my performance be measured?
> What type of mentoring program does the company offer?
> What are the opportunities for professional growth?
> How do you see me helping you to meet the challenges you're facing?
> How well do you think I'd fit into this job?

Use the following exercise to create your own questions that you can ask during interviews.

Questions I Can Ask During Interviews

Purpose: To develop questions to ask a prospective employer during an interview.

1. _____
_____
_____
_____

2. _____
_____
_____
_____

3. _____
_____
_____
_____

4. _____
_____
_____
_____

5. _____
_____
_____
_____

Handling Typical and Tough Interview Questions

Interviewers have typical and sometimes tough questions they usually ask job candidates. How you handle the questions is vital.

Be certain to listen actively to the questions. You want to be sure to answer the question asked not the question you thought you heard. Answer a question with a question especially if you're not sure what information the interviewer is seeking.

If you've done your homework—you know yourself and what you want to achieve and you've researched both the company and the job—you'll be able to handle any question that's thrown at you. Here are some common interview questions, from typical to tough, and suggestions for ways you can handle them. Typical interview questions include:

> *What can you tell me about yourself?* There's no right answer to this question, but since it's always asked you should have a plan for answering it so that your response puts you in the best light. You could start with highlights of your basic life history told in chronological order, spotlighting some of the past jobs you've held and strengths you bring to the workplace. Or you could paint an impressionistic portrait of yourself such as, "I'm someone who moves into new situations and gets things started. Everything I've done for the last five years . . ." Whichever way you choose, make certain that you include a description of your skills—"I write quickly and easily"—and link each skill to an example from your work experience. Make sure that your answer is brief and concise. The interviewer isn't interested in a 40-minute monologue.

> *Why do you want to work for us?* From the research you've conducted about the company, pick two or three good reasons for wanting to work there. For example, maybe your research has uncovered that the company plans to open a new branch office. You might mention that and add, "I'm very much interested in being part of a company that's expanding."

> *Where would you like to be five years from now?* You know the answer to this because it's part of your long-term career strategy. If you can compare your goals with the growth possibilities of the prospective company, you'll breeze through this question. But avoid telling the interviewer that you'll be doing his or her job five years from now. That

may be an honest response, but it'll be perceived as a threat. Instead say something like, "I'd like to work with you, helping to grow this company."

➤ *What do you like best about your work?* Emphasize the elements you know will be part of the position. For example, if you know you'll be part of a work team say, "I enjoy the challenge of working and solving problems with a group of dedicated individuals."

➤ *What was your most difficult or complex project that was challenging to you.* This question tries to get at various managerial skills such as planning and organizing, interpersonal effectiveness, communication effectiveness, and so on. Be prepared to answer the question by explaining how you handled a project by setting priorities, resolving conflicts, overcoming obstacles. Use your experiences from previous work, school, extracurricular, community, volunteer, military, or personal experiences.

TIPS

There are a variety of other questions that may be posed to you during an interview. Be prepared to answer the following as well.

➤ Why did you enter your job field?
➤ What is the ideal job for you?
➤ Why did you pick your major?
➤ What courses did you like best/least and why?
➤ Have you had any special training for this job?
➤ What would you do to improve our company?
➤ Could I see samples of your work?
➤ What are your three greatest strengths?
➤ What are your greatest accomplishments so far?
➤ What are some of your outside interests and activities?

Tough interview questions can include questions similar to the ones that follow.

➤ *Why do you want to leave your current position?* Approach this potential minefield carefully. If you answer negatively—"My boss is a jerk"—the interviewer could think that you'd feel the same way about the boss at the new company, and if the interviewer is the boss-to-be, you've just sunk your chances of getting hired. Instead, answer the question positively: "I enjoy my present position, but it's time for me to grow. I also see this position as a way of using my background to help your company move ahead."

> *What are you looking for?* Job seekers often think that this question refers to salary, benefits, and perks, and if you respond that way, you've lost an opportunity to show how hiring you would be mutually beneficial. Instead, say something like: "I'm looking for a chance to realize my full potential through a real challenge," or "I enjoy being part of a problem-solving team that helps the company grow."

> *What is your greatest weakness?* Watch out for this one! This is not the moment for true confessions such as "I can't meet deadlines," or "I'm completely disorganized," or "Details bore me." The trick to answering this question is to come up with a weakness and turn it into an strength. For example, many people consider it a weakness to be a perfectionist, especially if the perfectionist is unable to meet deadlines. So if you view yourself this way, turn this weakness into a strength: "I'm a perfectionist. I like taking a project and working on it until I get the job done right, and I always meet my deadlines."

> *Why have you changed jobs so frequently?* Variations of this question include "Why are you unemployed?" and "Why have you been unemployed?" Be honest by giving the reasons for frequent job changes or for unemployment—focusing on positive rather than negative reasons. For example: "I regretted leaving my last position because the company was great to work for. Unfortunately, my hours were changed, which made it impossible for me to attend school. My boss and I agreed that completing my degree was more important."

> *Why should I hire you?* Since you know the requirements of the job, parallel the needs of the company to your top skills and qualifications. Cover the top three needs of the company and show how your background and experience make you perfect for the job.

> *What salary are you expecting?* Tactfully avoid answering this question early in the interview by saying something like, "While salary is an important issue, at this point I'm interested in learning more about how I would fit into this position." Then ask a question that will get the interview back on less volatile ground. By talking salary before you know about the job's responsibilities and the range of salary the company is offering, the salary figure you state may be too low or too high.

Use the following exercise to draft answers to three typical and three tough interview questions. Rehearse your answers before you go on an interview.

Typical Interview Questions and My Answers

Purpose: To develop answers to typical questions that are asked during an interview.

Question 1: What can you tell me about yourself?

My Answer: _____

_____

_____

_____

Question 2: Why do you want to work for us?

My Answer: _____

_____

_____

_____

Question 3: Where would you like to be five years from now?

My Answer: _____

_____

_____

_____

Tough Interview Questions and My Answers

Purpose: To develop answers to tough questions that are asked during an interview.

Question 1: What are you looking for?

My Answer: _____

_____

_____

_____

Question 2: What is your greatest weakness?

My Answer: _____

_____

_____

_____

Question 3: Why should I hire you?

My Answer: _____

_____

_____

_____

After all the typical and tough questions have been asked, the interviewer will close the interview. This can happen in one of three ways.

1. *The interviewer might thank you for your time* and tell you that you'll hear from the company after all interviews have been conducted. You can ask when you might expect to hear and make a note of this in your notebook.

2. *The interviewer might ask you to return for a second interview* or for an aptitude or medical test. Ask for details about any test you are asked to take. If you are invited back, jot the details of the appointment in your notebook.
3. *The interviewer might offer you the job.* If this happens, ask for a day or two to consider the offer, even if you know you really want the job. This gives you time to talk to other people and to think about whether the company, job, salary, and potential for growth mesh with your career objective and your long-term goals.

The All-Important Follow-Up Letter

No matter how the interview ends, you should send a brief letter to the interviewer, thanking him or her for taking the time to meet with you. Your letter will reinforce the points you made during the interview and will show your level of interest in the company and the job. Use the following samples to guide you in the writing of your follow-up letters.

Jesse Smith
23 First Street • Albany, NY 12208
(518) 555-3647 • jsmith@aol.com

February 15, 1999

Ms. Amee Wong
Human Resources Manager
Cutler & Quigley, Inc.
35 South Hills Road
Clifton Park, NY 12065

Dear Ms. Wong:

Thank you for taking the time to meet with me yesterday about the assistant accountant position at Cutler & Quigley, Inc. I believe my experience in bookkeeping, payroll services, tax preparation, and computer and interpersonal skills would contribute to the success of the position we discussed.

I was impressed with your company, and I believe I would be a valuable addition to your staff. I would appreciate your serious consideration of my candidacy for the assistant accountant position.

Thank you again for the opportunity to meet with you and to learn about your company. I look forward to hearing from you.

Sincerely,
Jesse Smith

Jesse Smith
23 First Street • Albany, NY 12208
(518) 555-3647 • jsmith@aol.com

February 15, 1999

Ms. Amee Wong
Human Resources Manager
Cutler & Quigley, Inc.
35 South Hills Road
Clifton Park, NY 12065

Dear Ms. Wong:
  Thank you for taking the time to meet with me yesterday about the assistant accountant position at Cutler & Quigley, Inc.
  Although we agreed that my qualifications are not in line with your needs at this time, I wanted to let you know how tremendously impressed I was by the quality of work being done at your company. Therefore, I hope you will keep me in mind should a more suitable opening occur.
  If you learn of other companies in need of talents like mine, I would greatly appreciate your bringing my resume to their attention.
  Thank you again for the opportunity to meet with you and to learn about Cutler & Quigley, Inc. I hope we will have the opportunity to meet again.

Sincerely,
Jesse Smith

  Now that you have a good overview of the interview process, use the role-playing exercise that follows to become comfortable and confident in an interview situation.

Interview Role-Playing

Purpose: To become comfortable and confident in an interview situation.

Choose a friend who is willing to play the part of the interviewer. Ask your friend to develop a list of interview questions to ask you.

_____

_____

_____

Prepare a list of responses to typical and tough interview questions.

_____

_____

_____

Enact a mock interview session.

_____

_____

_____

After the session, discuss how well you think you did during the interview. Ask your friend to evaluate your performance. What did you do well during the interview? What did you do that you could do better?

_____

_____

_____

_____

_____

_____

Second Interviews

If you made a strong impression in the initial interview, you may be called back for a second interview. Second interviews are often opportunities for managers in the company or the team members you'll work with to meet you. Treat second interviews just as you do first interviews and follow the same recommendations for giving a spectacular presentation. Don't get overconfident. Just because you've been called back doesn't mean you have the inside track to the job. The company may be calling back other candidates, too.

Second interviews can be less nerve-wracking because you're familiar with the company and the person who initially interviewed you. But if you have to face a number of individuals or an entire search committee, your knees will be knocking before you know it. Take a few deep breaths and visualize a successful encounter before you go in.

The questions you will be asked during a second interview tend to be focused more on the skills and abilities you can bring to the company. Be prepared by bringing copies of your portfolio and real-life examples from work with you. These will help to demonstrate how you've used your skills and abilities to accomplish what you've achieved in various areas. Strive to match your qualifications to the needs of the company and the specific requirements of the job.

Follow up a second interview with a note to the person who arranged the interview. Thank the person for his or her time and interest in you and mention your excitement at the possibility of joining the company. Then, cross your fingers and hope that the search committee selects you for the position.

The Results Are In

When You Are Not Selected for a Job

Unfortunately, you won't receive a job offer for every interview you go on. But you can use every interview as a stepping stone to the next one. Review your performance and make notes in your job search notebook. Use the following exercise to evaluate yourself.

My Interview Evaluation

Purpose: To evaluate your performance during an interview.

The interviewer seemed most impressed by

_____

_____

The interviewer seemed least impressed by

_____

_____

I did the following things well:

_____

_____

The following things I did need improvement:

_____

_____

I can make improvements by

_____

_____

When You Are Offered a Job

Hooray! The phone call from the company came, and the human resource manager offered you the job. You're thrilled! But don't accept just yet because some issues still must be worked out. The human resource manager will invite you to the company to discuss the aspects of the offer, including compensation, benefits, and details about the job itself. Use the Job Offer Checklist on the next page to make sure that all areas are covered and add any questions that pertain to your special circumstances.

In pressure situations, we tend to feel the tug to make snap decisions. When you are on the job, you will make these important decisions regularly based on your experience and wisdom. One area to never do this is right after you have been offered a new job. If the employer pushes you to make an instant decision, you should professionally request at least 24 hours to make a decision. Give yourself time to think things through—and complete the following exercises.

YOUR TURN

Job Offer Checklist

The salary is _____

Does the company pay for overtime?   ☐ Yes   ☐ No

What is the pay schedule?   ☐ Weekly   ☐ Biweekly   ☐ Monthly

Does the company offer a pension or investment plan?   ☐ Yes   ☐ No

Can I contribute to the pension or investment plan?   ☐ Yes   ☐ No

Does the company match my contributions?   ☐ Yes   ☐ No

The percentage matched by the company is _____

When do I earn vested rights in the plan? _____

Does the company provide tuition reimbursement?   ☐ Yes   ☐ No

The company's vacation policy is _____

The company's holiday/sick leave policy is _____

The company offers these insurance benefits: _____

The company dress code is _____

The standard work schedule is _____

Is flex-time an option?   ☐ Yes   ☐ No

I am expected to begin work on _____

The work I will be doing includes _____

Other areas of concern for me include _____

Assessing a Job Offer

Once the company has made its offer, you owe it to yourself to review it. The offer is the beginning of a business relationship, and you need to decide if this is the right relationship for you. Consider the following questions.

Is the job a good match for you? Probably the most important factor is your fit within the organization. Did you enjoy meeting the people who worked at the company? If you met your immediate supervisor, do you think that he or she is a person you'll feel comfortable working for? What was the climate of the company? Rigid or open? Decide whether there is an appropriate level of challenge to the position. Will you have the opportunity to participate in the kinds of activities you're interested in? Will the job provide the growth you'll need to meet your eventual career goals?

Will you have a mentor? Look for a job in which there will be someone who will take a personal interest in your professional career; someone who will give you the opportunity to try new or different things; someone who is supportive but candid with you.

Are there opportunities for advancement? No one wants to get stuck in a dead-end job. Look back in your notebook for the interviewer's answer to this question: What career opportunities exist beyond the entry-level position? The answer will give you information about the career path that leads out of the position you're considering. Does the job seem to hold promise for positions you would like to have?

What are the fringe benefits? Some desirable fringes include: employer-paid health and dental insurance, tuition reimbursement, pension or profit-sharing plan, company car, free parking, relevant seminars and symposiums, professional memberships, relocation assistance, and interim living expenses. What is important to you?

Is the salary in line with your skills and experience? Your library research has uncovered salary ranges for similar positions, but how does your own market value impact on that range?

Ask the human resource manager for a day or two to consider the offer. Then use the following exercise to determine what you want from a company.

My Company Wish List

Purpose: To determine the factors important to you for accepting a job.

List ten things that are important for you to have from a prospective employer. Your list could include a specific level of salary, challenging work environment, tuition reimbursement, etc.

1. _____
   _____

2. _____
   _____

3. _____
   _____

4. _____
   _____

5. _____
   _____

6. _____
   _____

7. _____
   _____

8. _____
   _____

9. _____
   _____

10. _____
    _____

Next, rank your list of ten things in priority order, assigning 1 to the thing that is most important to you and 10 to the thing that is least important to you.

1. _____

   _____

2. _____

   _____

3. _____

   _____

4. _____

   _____

5. _____

   _____

6. _____

   _____

7. _____

   _____

8. _____

   _____

9. _____

   _____

10. _____

    _____

Last, compare your prioritized list of things with the offer made by the company.

My List   **Their Offer**

 1. _____

_____

 2. _____

_____

 3. _____

_____

 4. _____

_____

 5. _____

_____

 6. _____

_____

 7. _____

_____

 8. _____

_____

 9. _____

_____

10. _____

_____

From these answers, you will be able to determine if this offer represents the right relationship for you. ■

The Art of Negotiating: Salary, Benefits, Perks

Even when you determine that the offer represents the right relationship, you shouldn't bite at the first package dangled in front of you. The name of the game is negotiating, and since the company definitely wants you, you have the power to get more of what you need.

If you know the range of salaries for the job in your industry and in your part of the country, you can judge how close the company's offer is to the minimum you were expecting. If you were expecting a higher level, you could respond by indicating a range you would consider. For example: "I believe that a salary range of between _____ and _____ fits both my experience and this job. I believe this because (cite your reasons). Don't you agree?" If the human resource manager agrees, you're golden. If not, you need to negotiate for a salary that you can both be comfortable with. Don't be greedy but do be sure you accept a salary that is in line with your skills and abilities.

Benefits and perks can sometimes be negotiated at some companies. At others, the benefits package is fixed and nonnegotiable. Ask the personnel director about the company's policy toward benefits.

If benefits and perks are negotiable, you need to look at the package and determine what you want or need in terms of fringes and perks. If the offer includes no vacation during the first year and two weeks in the second, you might negotiate for two weeks during the first year and three weeks thereafter. If the offer includes partial tuition reimbursement for any course you take, you might negotiate for total reimbursement for any course you take that is directly related to your job. Enter negotiations with the spirit of win–win, and you'll reach a compromise that works for both you and the company.

Responding to Job Offers

Declining a Job Offer

Sometimes the company doesn't have the flexibility to offer you more than is already on the table with the initial offer. Then you must decide if you should accept the offer just to have a job or if it would be better for you to continue job hunting. If you decide to continue job hunting, you must decline the offer. Do so promptly and professionally by telephoning the human resource manager and then by sending a follow-up letter, thanking the company for the offer and expressing your regret that you were unable to accept the position. Don't burn any bridges and leave the door open for future job possibilities.

Accepting a Job Offer

Once you have a final, attractive offer on the table, you'll be eager to accept the job. Let the personnel director know as soon as you have decided. The company may ask you to sign a letter of agreement that spells out the terms of employment. Review this letter carefully to make sure the terms represent accurately the items you negotiated.

The letter of agreement will also indicate the date and time you are to report for work. Circle that date on your planning calendar, sign the letter of agreement and pop it in the mail, then take some time to celebrate. You've landed a job, and you've taken a giant step on the path of your journey of a thousand miles.

ELEMENTS OF EXCELLENCE

Accepting an offer is only the beginning of your career. In this chapter you learned

> the various types of interviews you may face and how to prepare.
> what interviewers look for in a candidate.
> how interviewers treat candidates.
> how to shine during an interview.
> what to do after an interview.
> how to assess whether a job offer is right for you.

Step into Chapter 4 where you'll focus on the next step of your journey of a thousand miles—finding success through networking. ■

Read All About It!

Ball, Frederick W., & Barbara B. Ball. *Killer Interviews*. New York: McGraw-Hill, 1996.
Beatty, Richard H. *175 High-Impact Resumes*. New York: Wiley, 1996.

Besson, Taunee. *Cover Letters: Proven Techniques for Writing Letters That Will Help You Get the Job You Want.* New York: Wiley, 1995.

Betrus, Michael, & Jay A. Block. *101 Best Resumes.* New York: McGraw-Hill, 1997.

Eyler, David R. *Job Interviews That Mean Business.* New York: Random House, 1996.

Falke, Martha. *The First Four Seconds: Things Successful Men Know about Dressing for Power.* San Antonio, TX: Falcon House, 1991.

Farr, J. Michael, Sara Hall, & Susan Christophersen. *Why Should I Hire You: How to Do Well in Job Interviews.* Indianapolis, IN: Just Works, 1992.

Kennedy, Joyce Lain. *Job Interviews for Dummies.* Chicago: IDG Books Worldwide.

Koren, Leonard, & Peter Goodman. *The Haggler's Handbook: One Hour to Negotiating Power.* New York: Norton, 1991.

Krannich, Caryl, & Ronald L. Krannich. *Interview for Success: A Practical Guide to Increasing Job Interviews, Offers, and Salaries,* 7th ed. Manassas Park, VA: Impact Publications, 1998.

Lavington, Camille, with Stephanie Losee. *You've Only Got Three Seconds: How to Make the Right Impression in Your Business and Social Life.* New York: Doubleday, 1997.

McDonnell, Sharon. *You're Hired!: Secrets to Successful Job Interviews.* New York: Macmillan.

Marler, Patty, Jan Bailey Mattia, & Sarah Kennedy. *Job Interviews Made Easy.* Lincolnwood, IL: VGM Career Horizons, 1995.

Morgan, Dana. *10 Minute Guide to Job Interviews.* New York: Arco, 1998.

O'Malley, Michael. *Are You Paid What You're Worth?* New York: Broadway Books, 1998.

Yeager, Neil, & Lee Hough. *Power Interviews: Job-Winning Tactics from Fortune 500 Recruiters.* New York: Wiley, 1990.

Books I've Read

Use the space provided to list the books you've read in this subject area and to reflect on what you've learned from reading them.

1. _____

2. _____

3. _____

4. _____

5. _____

Internet Resources

http://www.collegeboard.org

The College Board has a career questionnaire on its Web site. Answer the questions and match yourself by ability, skills, and temperament to specific careers.

http://www.review.com

The Princeton Review site has a similar questionnaire and also contains job-hunting suggestions.

My Favorite Internet Sites

Use the space provided to list your favorite Internet sites.

1. _____

2. _____

3. _____

4. _____

5. _____

Chapter 4

≫≫≫≫≫≫≫

Success Through Networking

People who have dreams are people who are going some-where. "Somewhere" isn't a vague location because these people know exactly where they're headed. You can be among them, and they can help you along the way. That's what networking is all about. The golden rule of net-working is: Do more for others than they do for you.

> Do not surround
> yourself with
> people who do
> not have dreams.
>
> NIKKI GIOVANNI,
> AMERICAN POET

After completing this chapter, you should understand

> the definition of formal and informal networking.
> the win–win aspects of networking.
> how to be open to networking opportunities.
> how to promote yourself through taking action and getting involved.
> how to appreciate those who make your success a little easier.

In the computer world, a network links many separate PCs for optimal operation of an enterprise. In the business world, a network links many separate people for optimal performance in finding a job, forging a career, and focusing on life-long success.

What Is Networking?

Networking is the process of making, using, and retaining both professional and personal relationships with the goal of exchanging information or services among individuals, groups, or institutions. Through networking, you develop personal resources as a result of your ability to pay attention, take action, become involved, and show your appreciation for the positive gestures and actions of others.

Think of every encounter you have with another person as a form of networking. Be on your best behavior, be confident, be prepared to speak about your goals, and be willing to listen for ways you can assist other people in the achievement of their goals. You will find amazing benefits if you consistently practice networking strategies throughout your carreer.

Informal versus Formal Networking

Networking can be informal or formal. Formal networking takes place during informational interviews, when cold calling prospective employers, at career fairs, through internships, and while job shadowing. You can also find opportunities for formal networking at meetings of professionals in your field, at business-to-business exchange events sponsored by a local chamber of commerce, and during gatherings of your church or temple.

Informal networking can take place anywhere with anybody—your family and friends, those you know at school and at work, individuals with whom you share recreational or sporting activities, people you meet on-line, and other social and neighborhood contacts. For example, Alexis E. is a writer with a long-term career objective of becoming a screenwriter in Hollywood. She enhances her writing skills by taking credit-free courses in creative writing, nonfiction writing, and juvenile fiction writing at a local community college. Recently, Alexis signed up for a course in writing and publishing books.

"I thought it would be fun to learn about book publishing in case I want to turn one of my screenplays into a novel," Alexis said. On the first night of class, the instructor asked the students to introduce themselves and to tell why they had enrolled in the course.

"I gave my little spiel," Alexis said, "and included the fact that my ultimate goal was screenwriting and that I was looking for an agent. I knew it didn't fit within the scope of the course, but I threw it in anyway. As it turned out, one of the other students was originally from Los Angeles, where she had worked for an agent who handles screenwriters. She gave me his name and number and said that I could mention that she had referred me. I contacted him, he remembered her, and he agreed to read one of my scripts. It's not easy to get an agent, and I wouldn't have been able to make that connection on my own."

Jose R. works part-time in the shipping department of a large department store while finishing his four-year business degree. His career objective is to break into retail sales. At the store's staff holiday party, Jose introduced himself to the manager of the menswear department and spent some time discussing industry issues and the particular challenges of running a specialty department. "We had a terrific conversation, and I told him about my wanting to start a career in sales," Jose said. "A few weeks later I found a journal article that had some good ideas for handling one of the problems he and I had discussed at the party. I made a copy of the article and some notes about how a few of the ideas could be implemented at the store. Then I dropped it off at his office."

The manager appreciated Jose's initiative and ideas. He called Jose to thank him and to mention that when the next sales associate opening occurred he would let Jose know. "I felt great because my wanting to help him made him willing to help me," Jose said.

The Win–Win Aspects of Networking

Jose's comments point out the win–win aspects of networking. According to Stephen R. Covey in his best-selling book *The Seven Habits of Highly Effective People,* "Win–win is a frame of mind and heart that constantly seeks mutual benefit in all human interactions. . . . Win–win is based on the paradigm that there is plenty for everybody, that one person's success is not achieved at the expense or exclusion of the success of others."

Networking based solely on self-centered wants tends to be a lose–lose proposition. If your sole purpose in networking rests upon your own desires, you will soon be exposed. The benefits of networking and paying attention to the people and situations around you is to learn from what you're doing, to see the benefits and the win–win situations that can come if networking is conducted correctly.

Networking is conducted correctly when the golden rule of networking is applied: Do more for others than they do for you. It really is that simple. Over time, you will derive from networking only what you put into it. So, if you want someone to help you, help him or her first. That's when you get to win.

MICHELLE BUENAU-CICCONE, AT&T

Once you've accepted a position and started your job, you have a perfect opportunity to get to know people in the company and to begin building relationships by using your free time wisely. Michelle Buenau-Ciccone, Human Assets Leader at AT&T in Albany, New York, suggests that you go to lunch with people from different levels in the company from secretaries and receptionists to managers and vice presidents. "These individuals can get you involved in extracurricular activities in the office," Ciccone said. "When you get involved in golf tournaments, softball games, or community events, you get to meet people from various levels, and those relationships are important."

> Try to get involved in those things [outside activities] because you're going to meet people, not just in your field but in other industries as well.

In addition to becoming involved, Ciccone also suggests taking a leadership role in the activities you join. "It will show that you're being proactive," Ciccone said. "Don't just sit back and wait for people to come to you. Take five minutes every day and ask yourself, 'What are the proactive things that I can do that are not part of my job that will help me to be more successful?'

Your involvement in activities may require that you work extra hours each week, but Ciccone believes that the investment of those hours will contribute to your success. "First impressions count," she said. "If you start out doing a great job, both in your work and in your extra-work activities, you'll become known as someone who's a go-getter, someone who takes the initiative. You'll get recognition, and you'll meet people, not just in your field but in other industries as well."

For Ciccone, success is built one relationship at a time. What can you do today to begin building relationships that will add to your success? ■

Being Open to Opportunities

How do you network with people you don't even know? This is a common question best answered by relating business networking to a form of social networking you've probably experienced—dating.

Imagine that someone you'd like to meet and get to know catches your eye. You see this person every day, but the individual seems oblivious to you. What can you do to make a connection? You might begin by finding out something about the person—name, where the person lives, works, or other places the person frequents. You might determine if you have a mutual friend or acquaintance. You tap into any and all outside resources that will bring the two of you together in a social, academic, or work-related setting. As crazy as it may sound, this is networking.

Simple in theory, isn't it? In practice, networking isn't that difficult either. Networking is a skill learned as any skill would be, and the practice of networking starts by making a connection. Networking is really only a series of connections that form a network of people working toward the same goal. When all the connections are made, the network is up and running. Picture a million people networking with each other. What do you think that can do for you and for them? Plenty.

The more people who know and respect you based on your professional conduct, the better your chances for successful networking. Successful networking results when you know yourself—your goals, your strengths, and your weaknesses—and when you remain open for opportunities, when you see the potential for a relationship that might not be obvious on the surface. For example, perhaps you meet a computer programmer at a social engagement. If you aren't interested in computer programming, you might make the mistake of thinking that investing time in getting to know this person might not be of much value. But if you take the time to understand what this person does, who the individual works for, where the person went to school, you will probably discover information that might be useful in the future. Maybe the person works for a company that interests you. Perhaps the person has friends working for companies in which you are trying to gain access. Maybe the person knows the hard-to-reach human resource manager at one of your prime company targets.

Be an opportunist. Look beneath the surface and do some conversational probing in a nice and friendly manner. At a minimum, you'll get to know someone better. Quite possibly that brief conversation could lead you right through the door of your next employer.

Be an exchanger of business cards. Keep plenty of your own handy and offer one at the end of a conversation. Most likely the person will reciprocate.

While you are handing out business cards, make sure you ask for and keep all the cards you acquire. In fact, consider getting a business card portfolio, which is a vinyl folder containing slots for the safekeeping of the cards you collect. Before you store each card, jot a note on the back that will refresh your memory about the person. For example, you might indicate the event at which you met the person, the name of a friend you have in common, or a special interest the person mentioned. The business card becomes an immediate and invaluable source for follow-up that helps you build the relationship.   ∎

Promoting Yourself

Part of relationship building is practicing follow-up and at the same time promoting yourself. After meeting someone, send a letter indicating how pleased you were to have met and how much you enjoyed the conversation. Drop a business card into the envelope. Receiving a letter and card may prompt the person to call you with a job lead or an invitation for lunch.

If not, you can be proactive. Review your collection of business cards and the notes you made on the back, looking for follow-up opportunities. For example, maybe someone you spoke to admired your briefcase and asked for information on where to get one like it. Pick up the phone and say, "Hello, this is _____. We met at the chamber's business mixer last week, and you were interested in a briefcase like mine as a gift for your brother. I dug into my files and found that I bought it at Cedar's Luggage Shop in the downtown mall last year. The style number is 763545. I hope that helps you." Thoughtfulness such as this will make the person remember you positively, and you never know how this will benefit you in the long run.

As the months roll by, you can nurture relationships by keeping in touch with people you've met. Make quick phone calls to share good news or, if you've had a particularly difficult time, call to ask advice. Your willingness to share your victories as well as your concerns causes people to be involved in your career and feel a vested interest in your future success.

Paying Attention

Just as you expect people to listen to you, you should be prepared to listen and to pay attention to those who contribute to your life.

When making new acquaintances, one of the biggest mistakes people make is not remembering names. You've probably had the experience of walking into a room, meeting someone and shaking hands, hearing the person's name, and then, seconds later, you realize you've forgotten the name you just heard. You wrack your brain trying to remember, then admit defeat and feel forced to say: "I'm sorry. Would you tell me your name again?" Talk about embarrassing.

Remembering names is an important part of the initial stages of networking and shows that you are paying attention and are interested in the individual you've just met. If you can walk into a room, meet ten people and leave hours later, saying good-bye to each person using his or her name, people will be astonished. Plus, they will remember you.

To avoid the embarrassment of forgetting someone's name, try these strategies.

Memory Strategy 1. Upon meeting someone, make a point to say his or her name aloud at least three times during the conversation. The best time to do this is when asking a question. For example: "Where do you work, Lorraine?" This will allow the person's name to be deposited in your memory banks.

Memory Strategy 2. When you meet someone, focus on something distinctive about the person. Is he wearing a flowered yellow tie? Does she have a red bow in her hair? Does she have bright blue eyes? Are his hands large? The first thing you notice about a person can be anything at all—something temporary such as clothing or jewelry the person is wearing or something permanent such as a striking physical feature, gestures, or body language. Then you need to associate the distinctive feature with the person's name. For example: Miss Red Bow = Mary.

Memory Strategy 3. Upon meeting someone, break down the person's name into syllables then think about the sound of each syllable. What images do the syllables trigger for you? For a simple name such as Bill, you might think of the image of a dollar bill. Or the name Mike might make you think of the image of a microphone. For longer names, think of multiple images. For example, the name Nicole may make you think of the image of a nickel or the image of a nick on a piece of coal. The name Wallace may make you think of the image of a walrus or the image of a wall with lace on it. Turn the name into the image, and you'll burn the name into your memory.

Memory Strategy 4. This strategy builds on the three previous ones. When you meet a person, say his or her name at least three times during the conversation. Focus on a distinctive feature and associate that feature with the person's name. The previous example was: Miss Red Bow = Mary. Then think about the sounds of the syllables in the person's name. Ask yourself what the sounds make you think of. For example, the name Mary might make you think of Merry as in Merry Christmas. Then think of an action that combines the distinctive feature and the image created by the sound of the person's name. You might think of tying red bows all over a merry Christmas tree. When you see that person again, even if she isn't wearing her distinctive bow, the image that will pop into your mind will be one of tying red bows all over a merry Christmas tree, and you'll remember her name—Mary.

By remembering names, you've achieved the first step in networking. A common trait among people is that they like to hear the sound of the their own name. This gives them a comfortable feeling and makes them feel friendly toward the person speaking the name. They will warm up to you and tell you a bit about themselves, and this is the start of building that business or social relationship, and all because you took the time to pay attention.

Being a "Networking Nag"

As has been mentioned, networking is an art, and in developing this art, there are some things that you do not want to do. While it is important to stay in contact with your network, do not suffocate them with your presence. Find a healthy balance between maintaining connections and remaining professional.

Taking Action

If you're going to sell a product, it seems only logical that you would want to know as much about the product as you can. While networking, you are the product, and although you might think that you know who you are and what you want to achieve, it's important to stay in tune with yourself at all times.

Practicing personal growth and improvement by knowing yourself is just as important as eating well, getting enough rest, and exercising regularly. Know your priorities and goals and review them every day.

If you don't make a concerted effort to stay focused on your priorities and goals, you'll have difficulty remembering them when you need them the most: when you have a chance meeting with the human resources director or one of the administrators of the company you're going after. You could easily lose an important contact or networking opportunity because you were caught up in an otherwise insignificant conversation and didn't notice points of the conversation that would have provided you with a chance to sell yourself.

For every person you meet, conduct a mental discovery process to find out as much as you can about each person: where the person works, for whom the person works, what the person does, the associations the person belongs to, who his or her friends are, and so on. Then think of your priorities and goals and begin to make connections that can prove to be mutually beneficial. Another strategy for taking action is to play a game called Benefactor Bingo. The game is fun, but it's also serious because winning the game will help you advance toward your goals. Here's how it works.

YOUR TURN

Benefactor Bingo

Purpose: To keep track of your various goals.

Compile a list of 16 traits, experiences, or pieces of information that you would like to gain over the next year. These could include developing into a great listener, meeting a newspaper executive, or understanding desktop publishing.

1. _____

2. _____

3. _____

4. _____

5. _____

6. _____

7. _____

8. _____

9. _____

10. _____

11. _____

12. _____

13. _____

14. _____

15. _____

16. _____

Create a Benefactor Bingo card (see the following sample) using each of sixteen traits, experiences, or pieces of information in a four-across and four-down arrangement. An aspiring commercial artist might have a Benefactor Bingo card like the following.

Find a Mentor in the Ad Business	Investment Advisor	Experienced Graphic Artist	Guest Speaker
Project Manager	Great Listener	Small Business Owner	Travel Agent
Ad Agency Executive	Newspaper Executive	Magazine Employee	Billboard Co. Employee
Book Publisher	Venture Capitalist	Young Attorney	Commercial Artist

Review your Benefactor Bingo card prior to attending any business or social function. Each time you meet someone who can help you meet the objective of one of the squares, place an X in the square. Each time you achieve BINGO (four in a row) reward yourself by doing something you enjoy.

Benefactor Bingo allows you to use to your advantage the serendipity of chance networking encounters. The next exercise asks you to plan proactively the encounters that will move you closer to your goals. ∎

Reach Out and Touch Someone

Purpose: To plan networking encounters.

Review the list you compiled for Benefactor Bingo—16 traits, experiences, or pieces of information that you would like to gain over the next year. For each item on your list, write the name and affiliation of any person you can think of who can provide the information you need. (It's not necessary that you already know the person. That's where the networking comes in.)

1. _____
2. _____
3. _____
4. _____
5. _____
6. _____
7. _____
8. _____
9. _____
10. _____
11. _____
12. _____
13. _____
14. _____
15. _____
16. _____

Think of three ways for you to approach each person on your list. You could include making an appointment to meet with the person, inviting an individual out to lunch, or attending a community event at which a person is likely to be.

1. _____
   a. _____
   b. _____
   c. _____

2. _____
   a. _____
   b. _____
   c. _____

3. _____
   a. _____
   b. _____
   c. _____

4. _____
   a. _____
   b. _____
   c. _____

5. _____
   a. _____
   b. _____
   c. _____

6. _____
   a. _____
   b. _____
   c. _____

7. _____
   a. _____
   b. _____
   c. _____

8. _____

   a. _____

   b. _____

   c. _____

9. _____

   a. _____

   b. _____

   c. _____

10. _____

   a. _____

   b. _____

   c. _____

11. _____

   a. _____

   b. _____

   c. _____

12. _____

   a. _____

   b. _____

   c. _____

13. _____

   a. _____

   b. _____

   c. _____

14. _____

   a. _____

   b. _____

   c. _____

15. _____
    a._____
    b._____
    c._____

16. _____
    a._____
    b._____
    c._____

Last, choose one strategy that you will implement for each person on your list. Then set a deadline for accomplishing that strategy.

1. _____
    Deadline: _____

2. _____
    Deadline: _____

3. _____
    Deadline: _____

4. _____
    Deadline: _____

5. _____
    Deadline: _____

6. _____
    Deadline: _____

7. _____
    Deadline: _____

8. _____
    Deadline: _____

9. _____

   Deadline: _____

10. _____

   Deadline: _____

11. _____

   Deadline: _____

12. _____

   Deadline: _____

13. _____

   Deadline: _____

14. _____

   Deadline: _____

15. _____

   Deadline: _____

16. _____

   Deadline: _____

Getting Involved

Networking is a lot like scoring points in a hockey game. Players know that the more shots they take, the better their chances are of scoring a goal. The same is true for you.

The more you are out meeting people, talking to them on the phone, or communicating with them through e-mail, the better chances you'll have of finding those meaningful relationships that will assist you in becoming successful. So get involved!

Join a community organization, a club, or a religious group. Meet people with similar interests in the business or social communities. For example, if you are an aspiring artist, you might find out the organizations to which your local museum curator belongs. Community involvement sends a clear message that you care about where you live. When you are involved in the community, you'll achieve visibility. Other people who are concerned and who care will take notice. You'll find that your involvement will not only benefit you in terms of networking and making connections but will benefit the community, too. That's the heart of win–win.

Volunteering

At the heart of community involvement is the idea of giving back in appreciation for all you have. In addition to giving back, you will also gain. You will increase your community contacts and develop personal and business relationships.

Think about those who actively participate in most not-for-profit volunteer groups within any community. Who are they? The majority are individuals holding executive-level positions who bear impressive professional credentials. Imagine trying to get past the gatekeepers in the plush offices over which these executives rule. Ordinarily, someone just off-the-street can't do it! But if you are a volunteer, you can!

Volunteering levels the playing field. Around the conference table of a not-for-profit organization you will find people at the top of their careers, those just starting out, and individuals who fall somewhere in between. But in their roles as volunteers, each person is an equal. Each person has a chance to express ideas and opinions, and each person is listened to by the others. There is no better way to showcase your skills and abilities and to demonstrate your passions for what you truly believe in than as a volunteer. Not only will you give back something to the community, but you will grow your talents and be brought to the attention of others who will want to assist you in your career growth and your current employment. You can take your career to new heights.

To volunteer, first review your values and beliefs that you identified throughout the exercises in Chapter 1. Then make a list of five community projects in which you strongly believe. You might want to volunteer in your community's food pantry or become involved in a health association such as the American Red Cross or the American Cancer Society. You might decide to become a tutor in an elementary school. Use the following space to list the projects that appeal most to you.

I Feel Strongly about These Community Projects

Purpose: To identify five community efforts that you can become involved in.

1. _____

_____

_____

_____

2. _____

_____

_____

_____

3. _____

_____

_____

_____

4. _____

_____

_____

_____

5. _____

_____

_____

_____

After you have reviewed your values and beliefs and have identified appropriate community projects, the next step is to contact the local volunteer center or the agency you are interested in joining. Most communities have volunteer centers that will assist you in finding an organization with which you could build a relationship. Check your local telephone book for names and addresses of organizations and then list the information in the space provided.

Organizations I Will Contact

1. Name: _____
Address: _____
Telephone Number: _____
Contact Person: _____
Date I Made Contact: _____
Result: _____

2. Name: _____
Address: _____
Telephone Number: _____
Contact Person: _____
Date I Made Contact: _____
Result: _____

3. Name: _____
Address: _____
Telephone Number: _____
Contact Person: _____
Date I Made Contact: _____
Result: _____

4. Name: _____
Address: _____
Telephone Number: _____
Contact Person: _____
Date I Made Contact: _____
Result: _____

5. Name: _____

Address: _____

Telephone Number: _____

Contact Person: _____

Date I Made Contact: _____

Result: _____

Choose one or two of the projects to which you might devote your time and enter the volunteer arena with passion. With volunteering, you go forth with a passion that you're doing something right and making a contribution to the community. The community benefits, the organization benefits, and you benefit!

Appreciating Those Who Make Success a Little Easier

Everybody likes to know that their efforts are appreciated, so take the time to show your thanks to those who make your success a little easier. The simplest way to do this is by handwriting thank-you notes.

Set a goal of sending three thank-you notes every week. Send a note to each person you meet, to each person you speak with on the phone, to each person who gives you a job lead, to each person who provides a referral. Become a thank-you note nut! What you'll find is that people will remember that you cared enough to thank them.

To get you started, here are thank-you note samples that you can use in four common career-building instances when thank-you notes are appropriate.

1. *Telephone Contact Thank-You.* I appreciated the time you spent talking with me on the telephone. Time is such a precious resource in today's business world that I wanted to thank you for your generosity. I will keep you posted as I move forward with the suggestions you provided to me. Thank you again.
2. *In-Person Contact Thank-You.* I appreciated your taking the time to meet with me. I so enjoyed meeting you, and I thank you for the time

we shared in fruitful conversation. I gained a good deal of information about the industry, and I appreciated all your insight and advice. Thank you again for taking time to see me.

3. *Job Lead Thank-You.* I appreciated the job lead you shared with me. I have sent my resume to [name of company] and am awaiting word about setting up an interview. Thank you for thinking of me regarding this opportunity. I will keep you posted on my success with [name of company].

4. *Referral Thank-You.* I appreciated your referral to [name of person] at [name of company]. I spoke with Mr./Ms. [name] today, and I will be meeting him/her on Friday for an interview. I could not have made this marvelous contact without your assistance, and I thank you. I will let you know the results of our meeting.

  YOUR TURN

When You Wish to Send the Very Best

Purpose: To identify those who have helped you recently.

In the space provided, list the names of three people who have done something for you in the past few weeks. The favor can be big or small. For example, the friend or colleague who spent some extra time preparing you for a final or the career counselor who edited your resumé.

1. _____

2. _____

3. _____

Purchase a package of blank thank-you notes. Write a short note to each of the three people you listed. Use the previous samples as guides and use the space provided to produce a rough draft of each note. Take the time to let each person know what their favor meant to you.

Note #1

_____

_____

Note #2

Note #3

Continue to thank at least three people a week. With a stockpile of thank-you notes, set aside an hour to thank the individuals who have impacted your life positively. Don't wait. Go ahead and start now!

ELEMENTS OF EXCELLENCE

As you come to the end of this chapter, reflect on the success that is possible through networking. Formal and informal networking events allow you to achieve mutually beneficial business opportunities. By being open to those opportunities, you can promote yourself and your goals by taking action, getting involved in community groups or volunteer activities, and by appreciating those who make your success a little easier.

In this chapter, you learned:

> how to be open to and effectively create formal and informal professional networks.
> the win–win aspects of networking.
> how to promote yourself through taking action and getting involved.
> how to appreciate those who make your success a little easier.

Now step into Chapter 5 where your focus is success on the job—your next step on your journey of a thousand miles.

Read All About It!

Boe, Anne, & Bettie B. Youngs. *Is Your "Net" Working?: A Complete Guide to Building Contacts and Career Visibility.* New York: John Wiley, 1989.

Bunkley, Crawford B. *The African American Network: Get Connected to More Than 5,000 Prominent People and Organizations in the African-American Community.* New York: Plume, 1996.

Fraser, George C., George MacDonald Fraser, & Les Brown. *Success Runs in Our Race: The Complete Guide to Effective Networking in the African American Community.* New York: William Morrow, 1994.

Hadley, Joyce, and Betsy Sheldon. *The Smart Woman's Guide to Networking.* Broomall, PA: Chelsea House, 1997.

Holtz, Lou. *Winning Every Day.* New York: HarperBusiness, 1998.

Kramer, Marc. *Power Networking: Using the Contacts You Don't Even Know You Have to Succeed in the Job You Want.* Lincolnwood, IL: VGM Career Horizons, 1997.

Krannich, Ronald L., & Caryl Rae Krannich. *Dynamite Networking for Dynamite Jobs: 101 Interpersonal, Telephone, and Electronic Techniques for Getting Job Leads, Interviews and Offers.* Manassas Park, VA: Impact Publications, 1996.

Mackay, Harvey. *Dig Your Well Before You're Thirsty: The Only Networking Book You'll Ever Need.* New York: Doubleday, 1997.

Mandell, Terri. *Power Schmoozing: The New Etiquette for Social and Business Success.* New York: McGraw-Hill, 1996.

Roane, Susan. *The Secrets of Savvy Networking: How to Make the Best Connection for Business and Personal Success.* New York: Warner Books, 1993.

Tullier, L. Michelle. *Networking for Everyone: Connecting with People for Career and Job Success.* Indianapolis, IN: Just Works, 1998.

Vilas, Donna, Sandy Vilas, & Donna Fisher. *Power Networking: 55 Secrets for Personal and Professional Success.* Austin, TX: Mountainharbour Publications, 1992.

Books I've Read

Use the space provided to list the books you've read in this subject area and to reflect on what you've learned from reading them.

1. _____

2. _____

3. _____

4. _____

5. _____

Internet Resources

Use a search engine and the following key words to find information related to topics in this chapter: *networking, win–win, volunteering.*

My Favorite Internet Sites

Use the space provided to list your favorite Internet sites.

1. _____

2. _____

3. _____

4. _____

5. _____

Career Success Notes

_____
_____
_____
_____
_____
_____
_____
_____
_____
_____
_____
_____
_____
_____
_____
_____
_____
_____
_____
_____
_____
_____
_____
_____
_____
_____
_____

Chapter 5

Success on the Job

Excellence is at the heart of success on the job. When your family and friends support your vision, when you have the right on-the-job attitude, when you dress professionally, when you hone your communication skills, and when you manage your time, you're on your way to excellence.

After completing this chapter, you should understand

> how to obtain support for your job.
> how to cultivate the right on-the-job attitude.
> how to dress professionally.
> how to enhance the basic communication skills of listening, speaking, and writing.
> how to manage your time.

Your first day on a new job is both exciting and terrifying. You're eager to start, but you wonder how you'll fit in and if your skills can cut it in the real world. Take a deep breath, then jump in with both feet. You're going to be terrific!

> The secret of joy in work is contained in one word—*excellence*. To know how to do something well is to enjoy it.
>
> PEARL BUCK,
> AMERICAN NOVELIST

TIPS

Your Basic Needs

Abraham Maslow, a well-known developmental theorist, is known for the hierarchy of needs. An important element of his theory is that you need to fulfill your basic survival needs before you can excel in what you do. These basic needs include things such as getting enough sleep, eating well, and being healthy. While it may seem sophomoric, remember to do these things before your first day of work (get enough sleep, eat breakfast, and look healthy!). Remember, first impressions are powerful. ∎

Obtaining Support for Your Vision

You want to do the best you can at your new job because your performance will help you attain the goals you've set for yourself. One way that you can make sure that you do your best is to enlist the support of your family and friends.

Share with those close to you the goals you've established and the steps that you must take to realize those goals. When your family and friends realize how serious you are about attaining your objectives, they'll probably do whatever they can to support your efforts.

Maybe you need two hours of quiet time in the evening to work on a project. If you let your family know this, they might try to keep the noise level down or maybe they could make plans to be away from the house during that time.

When you socialize with friends, they'll probably ask how your job is going or ask about the progress you've made on your goals. Be honest. Friends can provide wonderful feedback— "Gee, it sounds like you're doing great!"—and can also give you encouragement when you need it—"Things are hectic now, but you'll get through it. Just hang in there!" And if they're really good friends, they may even give you a kick in the pants if they think you need one. Having support for your job and for your goals will mean a lot when the going gets tough. It means you'll always have someone to turn to. It means you're all in this together.

Knowing the Requirements of Your Job

On your first day on the job, you must have a clear understanding of the job's requirements. Sure, you know what duties you have to perform, but knowing a job's requirements goes beyond that. If the following topics aren't discussed with you during the first day, talk to your boss about them pronto:

> ➤ What are your specific goals and objectives for the next 6 to 12 months? What specific results are you expected to deliver?

- ➤ What are the most important leadership skills required for success in this position?
- ➤ How will you be evaluated? By whom?
- ➤ Who are the critical people or groups that you will need to rely on to perform your job effectively?

Before you can do your job well, you need to know what the job requires. And you need to know that you are indeed doing well. Ask people for feedback on how things are going. Don't wait for a formal performance review. By then, it might be too late to make a course correction.

Cultivating the Right on-the-Job Attitude

Your on-the-job attitude is important because it contributes to how well you'll fit into the work environment and determines how happy and successful you'll be there. Have a good attitude, and your boss and colleagues will know that you're a great match for the job. Have a bad attitude, and you're likely to feel not only the hot wrath of your boss, but the cold shoulders of your colleagues, too. Consider these suggestions for cultivating the right on-the-job attitude:

- ➤ *Observe the office environment.* You'll spend the first few days on the job figuring out who's who and how things operate. This will give you valuable clues about how to behave as you ease yourself into the new work environment. Research shows that groups tend to accept those who adopt their rules of behavior, or norms, and reject those who ignore them. So keep your eyes and ears open during your first week to find out, for example, the degree of formality in the office. Are workers on a first-name basis with higher-ups, or are managers addressed as Mr. or Ms.? You don't want to call the CEO Marie if everybody else calls her Mrs. Custy.
- ➤ *Adjust your enthusiasm.* You can't wait to roll up your sleeves and get started because you just know you're going to whip that place into shape in no time. Your first lesson in the new workplace is that you won't endear yourself to more seasoned employees by being an overzealous know-it-all. So temper your enthusiasm—at least during the first week!
- ➤ *Accept criticism positively.* Because you're new at the job, it's expected that you'll do work incorrectly, make mistakes, and blunder your way

through a sometimes steep learning curve. Avoid the tendency to become defensive or withdrawn when you receive feedback or criticism. Accept the criticism positively by (1) asking for specific information about what you did incorrectly; (2) thinking about what you've heard and giving yourself time to react; and (3) deciding whether the criticism is well-taken. If it is, consider what you can do to avoid making the mistake again.

> *Obey working-hour rules.* If work starts at 8:30 a.m., be there at 8:15 a.m. to get settled, grab a cup of coffee, and be ready to start on time. Same thing at the other end of the day—you work until close of business. And don't duck out early for, or return late from, lunch.

> *Respect company policies.* Many companies have policies that prohibit making personal telephone calls on business time. Other companies have policies regarding proper business apparel for employees. These policies are usually set forth in an employee handbook. Make sure you get a copy from the personnel office. Familiarize yourself with the policies in place at your company, then respect and follow them.

Assembling a Working Wardrobe

Once you've read and understood the company's dress code policies, you can begin putting together a working wardrobe. Observe the employees who look polished and follow their lead in building your own wardrobe. Not sure where to start? You may need the help of a personal shopper.

TIPS

The Personal Shopper

A personal shopper works as a consultant for your professional look. After you tell the personal shopper about your definite likes and dislikes, he or she completes a computerized preference file for you containing information regarding sizes, favorite colors, styles, and designers as well as vital statistics such as name, address, phone number, birth date, and hair and eye color. You then describe the garments you're looking for, the desirable price range, and then you both hit the sales floor. This can save you great amounts of time, and save you mental energy. ■

JULIE ROSENTHAL, Banta Integrated Media

Just doing a job is not enough to ensure success, according to Julie Rosenthal of Banta Integrated Media. "It helps to become involved in the inner workings of the company," Rosenthal said. "I know that some people within the company who have moved up and who have done really well happen to be the people who are also involved in helping to establish company policies or making suggestions to supervisors on how to improve customer service."

> "I think the most important thing initially is to find out if they're interested in what we're doing because we don't want anybody who just wants a job, we want somebody who's going to be excited about our company."

In order to go these extra miles, Rosenthal believes it's important that a person take a job that he or she will enjoy. "People can tell when someone's not happy, and when you're not happy, it does rub off on your work," Rosenthal said. "If you're not enjoying what you're doing, you're not going to want to stay late; you're not going to want to help the company get ahead."

Although many job seekers think that being chosen by a company is important, Rosenthal believes that more important is the job seeker choosing the company. "You really want to be happy," Rosenthal said. "If you're enjoying what you're doing, then you're going to give more naturally."

For Rosenthal, that's a clear case of win–win.

Basic Communication Skills

Motivational expert Anthony Robbins believes "[t]he level of success that you experience in life, the happiness, joy, love, external rewards, and impact that you create, is the direct result of how you communicate to yourself and to others. The quality of your life is the quality of your communication." Your ability to communicate affects your level of success on the job, too. At work, your ability to listen actively, to speak well, and to create clear written messages reflects not only on you but on the company you work for. That's why good communication skills are so important.

Communication can be verbal or nonverbal, and the goal of communication is to exchange messages. The message flows from a sender (the person who transmits the message) to the receiver (the person who gets the message). Communication is considered effective when both the sender and the receiver have a common understanding of the message. That means when you (the sender) telephone your friend (the receiver) and say, "Let's go out for pizza tonight" (message), you both show up at the right place and the right time to split a pie. Even a simple message like this requires good speaking and listening skills.

Listening

Chapter 3 discussed techniques for active listening during job interviews, including being prepared to listen, being open and curious, and asking questions. Once you're on the job, you'll need to take listening to the next level by focusing on "listening between the lines" or paying attention to nonverbal cues. Many nonverbal cues are things you see when you look at a speaker:

> *facial expressions*—smiling, frowning, raising eyebrows
> *eye contact*—looking downward, making direct eye contact, glancing away
> *body language*—yawning, tapping fingers or feet, gesturing with hands

These cues give you a sense of the speaker's feelings and unsaid messages, and they improve your ability to understand the message.

You can test this by comparing a face-to-face conversation with a telephone conversation. Talking to someone in person lets you see the smile, the glancing away, and the hand gestures plus hear the voice. On the phone, you can only hear the voice, and that reduces your ability to understand the message. During the next few days, try the following exercise.

I'm Trying Hard to Hear You

Purpose: To compare the effectiveness of a face-to-face conversation with a telephone conversation.

Face-to-Face Conversation: When a friend shares an opinion or feelings with you, listen with your ears *and* with your eyes. When your friend finishes speaking, say, "Let me verify that I heard what you said . . ." and then say in your own words the message you think your friend communicated. Ask your friend to check the accuracy of your understanding. Use the space provided to write a short paragraph about your experience, indicating how close your understanding of the message was to your friend's actual message. If differences occurred, why do you think they happened?

_____

_____

_____

_____

_____

Telephone Conversation: When a friend shares an opinion or feelings with you, listen with your ears. When your friend finishes speaking, say, "Let me verify that I heard what you said . . ." and then say in your own words the message you think your friend communicated. Ask your friend to check the accuracy of your understanding. Use the space provided to write a short paragraph about your experience, indicating how close your understanding of the message was to your friend's actual message. If differences occurred, why do you think they happened?

_____

_____

_____

_____

_____

Speaking

Think of all the ways you communicate on the job by speaking. You give directions, ask and answer questions, explain procedures, share your ideas in meetings, and talk on the telephone. While people get their first impression of you from your appearance, they get their second impression from how you speak. If you want people to think of you as intelligent and competent, you must speak well.

TIPS

To guide you in your desire to speak effectively, keep the following aspects in mind:

> ➤ control the qualities of your voice—volume, pitch, rate, and tone
> ➤ pronounce words correctly and enunciate
> ➤ speak clearly
> ➤ use correct vocabulary and grammar

To determine how well you speak, tape record a conversation you have with a colleague. Play back the tape and listen to what your voice sounds like. Then ask a person you trust to listen to the tape and to evaluate how well you speak by using the following exercise.

YOUR TURN

How You Rate My Speech Qualities

Purpose: To evaluate speech qualities.

1. I speak standard English.   ☐ Yes   ☐ Sometimes   ☐ No

2. I speak at a moderate volume (not too loudly or too softly).
     ☐ Yes   ☐ Sometimes   ☐ No

3. I speak at a moderate pitch.   ☐ Yes   ☐ Sometimes   ☐ No

4. I vary the pitch for different meanings.
☐ Yes   ☐ Sometimes   ☐ No

5. I use pauses to emphasize important points.
☐ Yes   ☐ Sometimes   ☐ No

6. I control the tone of my voice.   ☐ Yes   ☐ Sometimes   ☐ No

7. I speak clearly and distinctly.   ☐ Yes   ☐ Sometimes   ☐ No

8. I use a wide range of words when I speak.
☐ Yes   ☐ Sometimes   ☐ No

9. I pronounce words correctly when I speak.
☐ Yes   ☐ Sometimes   ☐ No

10. I use correct grammar when I speak.   ☐ Yes   ☐ Sometimes   ☐ No

For any statements that you answered No, refer to some of the books at the end of this section, which can help you improve in those areas. ▪

Effective Conversations

Speaking well is only one part of effective conversations. Along with knowing what it is you want to say, you must

> ➤ establish a good environment for the conversation.
> ➤ use body language correctly.
> ➤ listen actively.
> ➤ allow others to speak.

That's a lot to pack into any conversation, but it all begins with the message—what you want to say. Be mentally prepared to deliver the goods by deciding the points you need to cover and your specific approach. Also keep in mind that in addition to knowing what you want to say, you have to remember what you don't want to say. You must respect confidences and be discreet and tactful. If not, people will view you as untrustworthy and rude. Not a reputation you want to have.

Establishing a good environment for conversation means you encourage the free flow of communication. You eliminate barriers by coming from behind a large desk, you sit with a person who is seated, you rearrange the furniture to make conversation comfortable. You also use positive body language—smiling, maintaining eye contact, gesturing for emphasis. Avoid any mannerisms that can be distracting to the other person such as shifting an object from one hand to the other or knocking a pencil against a coffee cup.

You listen actively, and you allow others to speak. Because a conversation is a dialogue not a monologue, you'll want to pay attention to your listener. Listeners give cues that tell you when they want to say something. Mind the cues, complete your statement, yield the floor, and then listen in silence.

Speaking on the Telephone

Because the visual dimension of the communication is missing, telephone conversations are challenging. You rely on your words and voice to send your message, and you have to concentrate on being courteous and attentive. Telephones, voice mail, and answering machines are integral parts of your job, so it pays to know how to use them in order to make your communication more effective.

> ➤ *When you place a call, greet the other person and identify yourself.* For example, "Good morning! This is Leo Sevigny from the Evergreen Consulting Group." This eliminates confusion for the person on the other end of the line—he or she doesn't have to try to guess who you are from the sound of your voice.
> ➤ *Speak directly into the mouthpiece of the telephone,* keeping your mouth about an inch from the phone. If the phone slips below your chin, the listener won't be able to hear you clearly, or your voice may not record clearly on a voice-mail system or an answering machine.
> ➤ *Be courteous* with the words you use and the tone of your voice. Remember to say "please" and "thank you," and to keep your voice pleasant and friendly.
> ➤ *Be attentive.* Acknowledge that you are paying attention by saying "Yes" or "I understand."

➤ *If you have to step away from the phone,* excuse yourself from the listener and then put the call on hold.

➤ *Have a pad of paper and a pencil near the telephone* in case you reach a voice-mail system instead of a person. You can jot down the menu choices, so you can be sure to choose the best one: "For account balances, press 2."

➤ *When leaving a voice-mail message,* be brief and to the point. A good rule of thumb these days is to be prepared to leave a voice-mail message before you make a call. This will help you to be concise if you should get the person's voice-mail box.

➤ *What you say can and will be used against you!* Remember that voice mail is no different than a memo. It can be saved and filed, so be careful of what you say. This is especially true when leaving messages for your peers and friends. Many organizations have personnel who check voice-mail messages when others are out of town. So you don't want to say anything that could embarrass you or cause problems for your friends.

➤ *If you get lost in an automated telephone system,* remember to press 0 to be put through to a human being.

➤ *For your own voice mail,* keep your recorded message brief, up-to-date, and professional. Some companies require employees to update their voice mail daily so that callers will know whether to expect a return call that day.

➤ *Check your voice mail frequently and return calls promptly.* Treat your calls as if each came from your boss.

Conversation Stoppers

There are some conversation stoppers that you should be aware of, and avoid at all costs. Some of these pitfalls include:

In person-to-person conversations

➤ be careful not to lose track of the conversation and repeat recently stated things.

➤ don't utilize risqué racial comments or statements.

> understand the importance of comfortable physical proximity to others.
> be aware of bodily functions such as belching and coughing.

In phone conversations

> avoid dropping the receiver or banging it on your desk.
> use speakerphone sparingly.
> if you have a cough, cover the receiver or move your head away.
> don't shout or mumble.

Writing

Letters, memos, e-mail messages, reports, and the like are all part of the writing tasks you'll do on the job. Are your written messages confusing and incomplete? Do you tend to overwrite? Does your boss go berserk with a red pencil on any written material you turn in? If so, do you fear that you'll have to repeat English 101? Relax! Writing is a skill that can be developed without going back to the classroom.

A classic book on the subject is *The Elements of Style* by William Strunk Jr. and E. B. White. Buy this book! This little gem will refresh your memory about usage rules, principles of composition, and an approach to style.

Once you recall the basics, apply the rules to the next memo you have to write. Then, as long as you're not on a deadline, put the memo aside for a day or two. When you go back to the memo after two days, read it through carefully. Put a mark in the margin next to anything that does not seem quite correct. Then pick up *The Elements of Style* and figure out how you can make the memo better. The secret to good writing is in rewriting, and *The Elements of Style* can help you make your writing sparkle.

Follow the same basic rules when writing e-mail messages but add a few for this special medium of communication:

> *Maintain a professional tone in all business-related e-mail.* Treat e-mail as a formal, written letter. You never know who'll be printing and saving the message or checking your grammar and punctuation. If you're even considering sending an e-mail that can be construed as contentious or creating conflict, think again! If in doubt, don't send the e-mail; talk to the person first.

➤ *Be brief.* People are very busy, and some receive hundreds of e-mail messages a day. Edit your e-mails so that they're brief and to the point.

➤ *Use emoticons when appropriate.* Emoticons are communication elements inserted in e-mail as a form of shorthand to represent phrases or to express emotions that may not come through in the words themselves. These are best used in personal e-mails, and not at your place of business. Some commonly used emoticons include:

BTW	by the way
CAM	couldn't agree more
FWIW	for what it's worth
FYI	for your information
GMTA	great minds think alike
ICBW	I could be wrong
IMO	in my opinion
IOW	in other words
ITA	I totally agree
JMO	just my opinion
LOL	laughing out loud
OTOH	on the other hand
<G>	grin
:-) or :)	smiley face (happy)
:-(	sad face (disappointment)

➤ *Read the message at least twice before hitting the Send button.* Does the message say what you want? Can any of the words be misinterpreted? Is the tone professional and appropriate? Once you've sent a message, there's no way to get it back.

➤ *Be polite.* Remember that you never know where an e-mail message will end up. Be proud to have that document in someone's file folder somewhere. Remember, too, that even though you delete e-mail from your directory, the message is still in your company's system and can be retrieved. Make certain that your e-mail doesn't contain anything you wouldn't want a third party to see.

Managing Your Time

"Those who make the worst use of their time are the first to complain of its shortness," according to 17th-century French writer Jean La Bruyere. Things may have been busy back then, but they're turbocharged today, and people complain more than ever that time is a dwindling natural resource. True, you can't control the passage of time, but you can take action to control your use of time.

Do you put things off? Do you complain about not having enough time for all you have to do? Do you waste or misuse time? If so, time management can help you overcome these obstacles to accomplishing your goals.

Procrastination

Chapter 1 characterized procrastination as a pothole in the road to success. People who put things off are called procrastinators. Many procrastinators delay tasks because they fear failure. They don't know how the task will turn out, and this uncertainty causes increased stress. So instead of plunging into the project, they come up with excuses for not starting it. Other procrastinators think that making a decision to undertake a task is just as good as completing the task. They decide to work on a project but then reason that they'll engage in personal tasks first and work on the project later. Somehow the project doesn't get completed.

Some people are happy to live their lives as procrastinators. If you have a tendency to put things off, and you're unhappy with the fact that you're not meeting your goals, make a decision right now to overcome procrastination.

Once you banish procrastination from your life, you'll start a task on time, work on it steadily, and finish it on time. You'll gain a feeling of control over projects. You'll meet rather than miss deadlines, you'll keep your stress level low, and you'll get things done. Think of the rush of satisfaction you'll feel when you complete a difficult project. What a feeling!

Beat procrastination by putting into practice these strategies for any task you've been putting off.

> ➤ *Set a deadline.* Decide when a task needs to be completed and use that as your deadline date. Circle that date on your calendar in red.
> ➤ *Break the task into its component parts.* You wouldn't eat a six-foot sub in one sitting would you? No! You'd probably cut it up in sections and eat one section every day. It's the same thing with huge projects. Tackle a

big project one section at a time. Make a list of all the project's component parts and do one part at a time. The momentum you'll build along the way will keep you moving through the entire project.

> *Establish a start date.* Overwhelming projects that require a lot of effort need more than just a deadline for completion. Look at all of the parts of your project that must be done and decide how long each part will take. Then, working back from your deadline, figure out when you need to start the project in order to finish it on time. Circle that date on your calendar in blue.

> *Start with something easy.* If the task is tough, ease yourself into the project by starting with something easy. Once you've begun, you can shift into the harder parts of the task. The Roman poet Horace said it best: "He who has begun has half done."

> *Schedule progressive rewards.* For a large task, reward yourself for accomplishing various sections. Save one big reward for completing the entire task.

I Just Don't Have Enough Time!

Perhaps you don't procrastinate. Maybe you complain that you just don't have enough time for all you have to do, including family, household, school, work, and community responsibilities. There's an old saying that if you need something done, ask a busy person to do it. Busy people realize that we all have the same number of hours each week: 7 days a week x 24 hours day = 168 hours, and they make the most of those hours. How do you use your hours? If you'd like to find out, use the following exercise.

YOUR TURN

How I Spend My Time

Purpose: To identify how you use your time over the course of a week.

For the next week, use the following time log to record how you spend your time. List all activities, including commuting, running errands, watching television, and leisure time.

My Time Log

Time	Monday	Tuesday	Wednesday
7:00 am			
8:00 am			
9:00 am			
10:00 am			
11:00 am			
12:00 noon			
1:00 pm			
2:00 pm			
3:00 pm			
4:00 pm			
5:00 pm			
6:00 pm			
7:00 pm			
8:00 pm			
9:00 pm			
10:00 pm			
11:00 pm			
12:00 midnight			
1:00 am			
2:00 am			
3:00 am			
4:00 am			
5:00 am			
6:00 am			

Thursday	Friday	Saturday	Sunday

Wasting and Misusing Time

People who complain about not having enough time for all they have to do often suffer from the twin problems of wasting time and misusing time. They waste time by slowpoking their way through projects, and they misuse time by spending too much of it on unimportant tasks and not enough of it on tasks that are significant. They end up spending days focused on trivial matters with no time left for the things that really matter to them. Don't let this happen to you! Use the following exercise to see how well you use your time. ■

How Well I Use My Time

Purpose: To identify how well you use your time.

Review the time log you kept for one week then complete the following:

The total number of hours I spent on these activities:

Sleeping: _____

Eating: _____

Working: _____

Commuting: _____

Chores: _____

Exercising/Recreation: _____

Socializing: _____

Watching TV: _____

Goofing Off: _____

Other: _____

Total should be 168 hours.

The total number of hours I spent on worthwhile activities: _____

_____

The total number of hours I spent on meaningless or trivial activities:

_____

The activities I wish I had spent more time on are

_____

_____

_____

_____

_____

The activities I wish I had spent less time on are

_____

_____

_____

_____

_____

The activities that I wanted to do but didn't get around to doing during the week are

_____

_____

_____

_____

_____

_____

Parkinson's Law states that "work expands so as to fill the time available for its completion." In the past, you've probably experienced the results of this law, but now you probably realize that without some sort of time management system, your time will evaporate. If you allow procrastination to eat away at your days, you will have lived a life without accomplishing any of your goals. Control your life! Achieve your goals! Take charge of your time!

Organization Is Key

Being organized means you keep your goals in mind and you plan to accomplish those goals in advance. You practiced being organized in Chapter 1 when you created short-, intermediate-, and long-term goals. You probably remember that planning comes before action, which is why you set up a plan for achieving the goals you set. As you developed your action plan, you decided what you want to do; considered the resources you need to do it; and outlined the steps you must take to achieve it. That's great! But you probably have more than one goal. How do you decide what you will spend your time on? You do that by setting priorities.

When you set priorities, you decide the tasks that are most important and which must be done first. Review everything you need to do and then allocate your tasks to one of the following four categories:

1. the tasks that must be done immediately
2. the tasks that are important to do soon
3. the tasks that can be delayed for a few days
4. the tasks that can be delayed for a week, a month, or longer

This system sets up your priorities. The tasks in categories 1 and 2 have the highest priority, and you should work on these first. The tasks in categories 3 and 4 have lower priority and can be done once you've accomplished the higher-priority objectives.

You'll find that establishing priorities helps you to isolate the most urgent tasks associated with particular goals. Sometimes you must postpone working on one or more of your goals so that you can attain the others. Practice setting priorities in the following exercise.

YOUR TURN

My Priorities for the Week

Purpose: To identify your highest priority activities for one week.

Make a list of all the things you have to do for the week ahead.

1. _____

2. _____

3. _____

4. _____

5. _____

6. _____

7. _____

8. _____

9. _____

10. _____

11. _____

12. _____

13. _____

14. _____

15. _____

16. _____

17. _____

18. _____

19. _____

20. _____

Review your list and assign each task a priority number from 1 to 4. Remember that 1 represents tasks that must be done without delay (highest priority); 2 represents tasks that should be done soon (important); 3 represents tasks that can be done next week (less important); 4 represents tasks that can be delayed for more than a week (least important). Now allocate each task to its place in the exercise My List of Tasks for the Week.

My List of Tasks for the Week

Week of: _____

1. The tasks that must be done immediately are

   _____

   _____

   _____

   _____

2. The tasks that are important to do soon are

   _____

   _____

   _____

   _____

3. The tasks that can be delayed for a few days are

   _____

   _____

   _____

   _____

4. The tasks that can be delayed for a week, a month, or longer are

   _____

   _____

   _____

   _____

Time Management Tools

Once you know your highest priorities, you can use time management tools to help you set up a schedule. Plug in your fixed daily activities such as working, attending class, sleeping, eating, and so on, then use the time left over for your highest priority tasks.

When scheduling those tasks, be realistic about the time involved for each activity. For example, if you need to spend 1 hour at the library researching a project, figure in the travel time to and from the library. If it takes you

30 minutes to get to the library, you'll need to allocate 2 hours for the research project (1 hour research time + 1 hour for round-trip travel).

Be aware of your peak energy levels throughout the day. Some people have high energy in the morning and are dragging by afternoon. Other people have to be blasted out of bed in the morning, but by afternoon they are going at full throttle. Schedule hard or important tasks for the times during the day when your energy is at its peak.

Your Planner

Time management tools, also called planners, are calendars in a variety of formats that help you schedule your life weeks and months in advance. Head to your local office supply store to check out the different types, styles, and sizes of planning systems that are available.

Select your system wisely. Because the planner will be your only source of information about your work, school, and social schedules, the system should have enough room for you to write and be a convenient size for you to carry with you. Some planners offer both paper-based and computer-based systems. Choose whichever type works the best for your lifestyle.

Many planners allow you to schedule intermediate- and long-term activities as well as to keep a daily To Do list. Your To Do list is the way you get things done that contribute to your intermediate- and long-term goals.

Get into the habit of creating your list the night before and itemizing all of the tasks that need doing during that day. Prioritize the tasks in A-B-C order with A-tasks being those of highest priority. If you have four A-tasks, you can further prioritize them by assigning A-1, A-2, A-3, and A-4 order to them. Consult your list during the day so that you know what you have to do, and cross items off your list when you've completed those tasks.

Use the following weekly planner to practice making time commitments for the next week. Start by entering your fixed daily activities such as working, attending class, sleeping, eating, and so on.

YOUR TURN

Weekly Planner

Purpose: To practice making time commitments for a week.

Complete the planner on the following pages.

My Weekly Planner

Time	Monday	Tuesday	Wednesday
7:00 am			
8:00 am			
9:00 am			
10:00 am			
11:00 am			
12:00 noon			
1:00 pm			
2:00 pm			
3:00 pm			
4:00 pm			
5:00 pm			
6:00 pm			
7:00 pm			
8:00 pm			
9:00 pm			
10:00 pm			
11:00 pm			
12:00 midnight			
1:00 am			
2:00 am			
3:00 am			
4:00 am			
5:00 am			
6:00 am			

Thursday	Friday	Saturday	Sunday

Now use the following space to create a To Do list of all the tasks you want to accomplish tomorrow. After you've listed them, assign each task a priority number from 1 to 4. Remember that 1 represents tasks that must be done without delay (highest priority); 2 represents tasks that should be done soon (important); 3 represents tasks that can be done next week (less important); and 4 represents tasks that can be delayed for more than a week (least important).

To Do List

1. _____

2. _____

3. _____

4. _____

5. _____

6. _____

7. _____

8. _____

9. _____

10. _____

Estimate the amount of time each of your highest priority tasks will take then list these tasks on the appropriate day of *My Weekly Planner*. As you complete your tasks, cross them off your To Do list.

Strategies for Managing Your Time

Benjamin Franklin wrote: "You may delay, but time will not." When you adopt time management tools that work for you, you'll be amazed at how easy it is to organize yourself and to make plans, schedules, and lists. But did you plan for the unexpected? That's hard to do, which is why time-planning tools often go out the window when life throws a curveball that introduces interruptions to your schedule.

If you want to harness the true power of effective time management, you must learn to be organized and flexible. That means you can handle interferences to your schedule, meet the demands of others, learn to say no when your time is already spoken for, and become skilled at using bits and pieces of time to your advantage.

Meeting the Demands of Others

Unless you live and work in a cave, you're surrounded by people, such as friends, family, and colleagues, who care about you and want some of your time and attention. Do you shut them out of your life just so you can maintain your schedule? No! You plan time in your schedule for socializing.

But what should you do when, even though you've planned social time, people interrupt you at other times? Simple—just plan to be interrupted. Build response time into your schedule by planning more time than you think a given task will take. In that way, you'll have plenty of time to finish a task by your deadline despite interruptions.

Just Say No

Realizing that you have only 168 hours a week to work with, you need to develop the ability to say no to extra projects or demands that will lead to overcommitting yourself. Explain to others who try to push the projects or make the demands that what you have already scheduled is important and that additional responsibilities have to take a number.

Now this will be difficult to explain to your boss, and that's where your time management tool comes to the rescue. When your boss comes into your office to toss more work into your in-basket, ask him or her for a few minutes of time to discuss priorities. Have available your time management tools and plans to share with your boss the work time commitments you already have scheduled. Then sort through the additional work that was placed into your in-basket. Ask your boss for help in prioritizing the new work. Your boss may realize that you are overcommitted presently and agree to shift the new work to a less hectic time. Or your boss may think that the new work is more important than your current projects and make the new work a higher priority. Whichever scenario plays out, you will continue to work on the highest priority projects, and you will not have your stress level rise because you have too much to do.

Using Bits and Pieces of Time

Occasionally, you will be presented with unexpected bits and pieces of time. Maybe a meeting gets out ten minutes early or perhaps a client cancels a one-hour appointment. What do you do with these bits and pieces? You use them.

When presented with such luxuries as extra time, immediately ask yourself: "What is the best use of this time right now?" Spend the time with small tasks such as catching up with your reading, getting some exercise, or starting a project. If you're an effective time manager you won't just kill time, you'll work it to death!

 ## ELEMENTS OF EXCELLENCE

As you come to the end of this chapter, consider the many factors involved in achieving success on the job. You need the support of family and friends, the right on-the-job attitude, and the right professional look. You need good communication skills in the areas of listening, speaking, and writing. You need to manage your time in order to reach your potential and to achieve your goals.

In this chapter you learned

- > how to obtain support for your job.
- > how to cultivate the right on-the-job attitude.
- > how to dress professionally.
- > how to enhance the basic communication skills of listening, speaking, and writing.
- > how to manage your time.

You're almost there, so keep going! Step into Chapter 6 where you'll look at achieving success for life.

Axelrod, Alan & Jim Holtje. *201 Ways to Manage Your Time Better.* New York: McGraw-Hill, 1997.

Benjamin, Susan. *Words at Work: Business Writing in Half the Time with Twice the Power.* Reading, MA: Addison-Wesley, 1997.

Booher, Dianna Daniels. *Get a Life without Sacrificing Your Career: How to Make More Time for What's Really Important.* New York: McGraw-Hill, 1996.

Covey, Stephen, A. Roger Merrill, & Rebecca R. Merrill. *First Things First.* New York: Simon & Schuster, 1994.

Gelb, Michael J., & Bradley L. Winch. *Present Yourself! Captivate Your Audience with Great Presentation Skills.* Rolling Hills Estates, CA: Jalmar Press, 1988.

Helgesen, Marc, & Steve Brown. *Active Listening: Building Skills for Understanding.* New York: Cambridge University Press, 1994.

Matthews, Candace & Phillip Edmondson. *Speaking Solutions: Interaction, Presentation, Listening, and Pronunciation Skills.* Upper Saddle River, NJ: Prentice Hall, 1994.

Moreno, Mary. *The Writer's Guide to Corporate Communications.* New York: Allworth Press, 1997.

Morrisey, George L., Thomas L. Sechrest, & Wendy B. Warman. *Loud and Clear: How to Prepare and Deliver Effective Business and Technical Presentations.* Reading, MA: Addison-Wesley, 1997.

Numrich, Carol. *Consider the Issues: Advanced Listening and Critical Thinking Skills.* Reading, MA: Addison-Wesley, 1995.

Strunk, William, & E. B. White. *The Elements of Style.* 3rd ed. Needham Heights, MA: Allyn & Bacon, 1995.

Swenson, Jack, & Elaine Brett. *The Building Blocks of Business Writing: The Foundation of Writing Skills.* Los Altos, CA: Crisp Publications, 1991.

Ratliffe, Sharon A., & David D. Hudson. *Communication for Everyday Living: Integrating Basic Speaking, Listening and Thinking Skills.* Upper Saddle River, NJ: Prentice Hall, 1989.

Venolia, Jan. *Rewrite Right: How to Revise Your Way to Better Writing.* Berkeley, CA: Ten Speed Press, 1987.

Williamson, Sarah. *Stop, Look and Listen: Using Your Senses from Head to Toe.* Charlotte, VT: Williamson, 1996.

Young, Pam, & Peggy Jones. *Get Your Act Together! A 7-Day Get-Organized Program for the Overworked, Overbooked, and Overwhelmed.* New York: HarperCollins, 1993.

Books I've Read

Use the space provided to list the books you've read in this subject area and to reflect on what you've learned from reading them.

1. _____

2. _____

3. _____

4. _____

5. _____

Internet Resources

http://www.eslcafe.com

Dave's ESL Cafe is a site with links to English-as-a-Second-Language resources on the Internet.

Use a search engine and the following key words to find information related to topics in this chapter: *listening skills, public speaking,* and *time management.*

My Favorite Internet Sites

Use the space provided to list your favorite Internet sites.

1. _____

2. _____

3. _____

4. _____

5. _____

Career Success Notes

_____

_____

_____

_____

_____

_____

_____

_____

_____

_____

_____

_____

_____

_____

_____

_____

_____

_____

_____

_____

_____

_____

_____

_____

_____

_____

_____

Chapter 6

Success for Life

The true measure of success is your own vision of a fulfilled life. Whatever your dreams may be, measure your success not by how far away you are from your goal but by how many steps you've taken toward your goal. With enough momentum—gathered from working with mentors, being a lifelong learner, and creating building blocks of commitment—you'll cease creeping along the path, and you'll soar to success. This chapter is your launching pad.

After completing this chapter, you should understand

> how mentors assist in achieving goals.
> how to find and work with a mentor.
> how to become a mentor.
> how lifelong learning contributes to life-long success.
> how to create building blocks of commitment to success.

Success is not a result or an ending point. It's a way of life. The way in which you go about moving toward your goals is important. If your life goal is to become the chief executive officer of a large international company, don't be disappointed if you're not offered the job on your first day of work. You need to be prepared for reality, especially the reality of the corporate world where patience is not only a virtue, it's also a prerequisite for the job.

> Never consent to creep when you feel an impulse to soar.
>
> HELEN KELLER, AMERICAN AUTHOR, LECTURER, HUMANITARIAN

Reality also means that much hard work is ahead of you. But if you're determined, if you'll let nothing stand in your way, you will successfully reach the end of the road. You have signposts to guide your journey—mentors, lifelong learning, and building blocks of commitment—so hold fast to your goals and keep your eye on the prize. You're on your way.

<156>

How Mentors Assist in Achieving Goals

Think about the idea of having a role model in your life for the you of the future. Imagine sitting down with this person to discuss your goals, dreams, and career plans and having this individual offer information, references, and guidance based on years of experience. This person—your mentor—is your ally in achieving your goals.

Mentors understand the industry, their part in the organization, and they have a great deal to teach you. If you are open to learning, mentors can share the things they did right, the mistakes they made along the way, and the benefit of their wisdom to help you avoid the same errors. Your mentor could be your boss, a colleague, a business partner, a friend, a parent, even a competitor. As you grow in your career and begin to network outside of your familiar surroundings, you'll meet many individuals who will bring an inspirational or educational influence to your life. Don't feel frustrated now if you have no one in your life who you feel fills the mentor roll. You've only begun to meet potential mentors.

As you grow professional and personally, you will be amazed at how your appetite for knowledge and your thirst for education will grow. What will also increase is your need for new mentors to support you as you enter new areas of your life.

You can have different mentors for various aspects of your career and/or personal life. You can even have the mentoring equivalent of a board of directors—multiple mentors from both inside and outside your company. You might also change mentors, depending on where you are in your professional development. From some mentors you may want inspiration and motivation; from others you may want discipline.

That's right, discipline. The best kind of mentor is one you will want to not disappoint. The best thing you can do for yourself is to tell your mentor exactly what you want in life. The funny thing about doing this is that afterwards, you'll feel that you don't want to let your mentor down.

Creating a Support Network

It's very easy to let yourself down. There will be times where you miss the deadline, botch an important presentation, or miss a detail. Especially in the early days of a new position, this can be self-defeating. First and foremost—do not get bogged down by early mistakes. If you tell a few people about your dreams and your vision, you'll have a much harder time explaining to them about your subsequent lack of progress. To avoid having to do that, you'll work harder, and you'll achieve success, and you'll be eager and proud to let your mentor know.   ■

Finding and Working with a Mentor

Rooted in ancient Greece, mentoring is a concept that's been given a modern-day spin by today's corporations. In Homer's *Odyssey*, when Odysseus went off to fight the Trojan War, he left his son Telemachus in the care of the tutor Mentor. Mentor later revealed her true identity—she was actually the Goddess Athena, patroness of the arts and industry—and went with Telemachus on his search for his missing father.

Similarly, your mentor should see you through thick and thin. But how do you find a mentor? Typically, you'll meet people who are potential mentors through work, as a result of your involvement in a business association, or through your community volunteer activities. (Are you starting to see how all of the topics discussed so far are starting to come together? That is why success is a lifestyle and not any one thing that you can put your finger on.)

Many companies today are updating the traditional one-on-one mentoring relationship with formal or guided mentoring programs. Through these programs, less experienced employees are matched with experienced, senior-level managers. Groups of protégés interact on a regular basis with a single mentor who may or may not be involved in the same department or business. In fact, the mentor may have very different talents and perspectives to bring to the table. This is called *cross-skill mentoring*, and as a result both the protégés and the mentor broaden their experiences and their knowledge bases.

In the years ahead, you'll find even more opportunities for formal or guided mentoring programs at companies interested in sharing so-called intellectual capital. In fact, a 1996 survey conducted by *Human Resource Executive* magazine found that between 1995 and 1996 the percentage of businesses planning mentoring programs more than doubled from 17 percent to 36 percent. Major corporations that have jumped on the mentoring bandwagon include AT&T, Merrill Lynch, Federal Express, General Motors, J.C. Penney, Bell Labs, DuPont, Sun Microsystems, Charles Schwab, BellSouth Corp., Barnett Bank, Texas Commerce Bank, and scores of others.

When choosing your mentor, be on the lookout for someone you admire who is open, successful, and someone you feel you trust and can turn to for advice. Other important characteristics include humility, the ability to listen, and an insatiable curiosity. Don't limit yourself to people just like yourself. Welcome diversity! Seek someone from a different ethnic group or of the opposite gender. (If you do select someone of the opposite sex, keep the relationship strictly professional.)

The courtship ritual for attracting a mentor is similar to the ritual of dating. Introduce yourself and if you seem to click with the person, invite him or her for coffee or a bite to eat, and the relationship flourishes or flounders from there. (If the relationship flounders after the initial get-together, don't blame yourself. Just because you're looking for a mentor doesn't mean that the person you've selected is interested in taking on the job.)

When the relationship flourishes, the person may invite you to attend a special program at his or her business association and then may ask to see some of the projects you're doing for work. He or she will make suggestions, offer advice, and provide moral support. You'll keep him or her posted by phone or e-mail on how you're doing, and you'll get together for lunch once a month where you'll exchange views about the business. Before you know it, your business friendship will evolve into a mentor-protégé relationship, and you will both be richer for it.

To make the most of that relationship, keep these guidelines in mind:

> ➤ *Understand your strengths and weaknesses.* This will help you and your mentor to create action plans that address areas of need.
> ➤ *Share your goals.* Your mentor can't help you achieve them if he or she doesn't know what they are.
> ➤ *Set an agenda.* Decide how much time you and your mentor will spend together and agree about what you will accomplish during those times.
> ➤ *Keep in contact.* Between the times you and your mentor get together, stay in touch through phone calls and e-mail. Tell your mentor about your progress and ask for help when you feel you're not making progress.

Becoming a Mentor

As you are enriched by being a protégé, you have the chance to enrich others by becoming a mentor. Don't think you have to be in your career for years before you share with others the knowledge you've gained. Even after only a year in your profession, you have a wealth of information to share with those coming up behind you.

Look for a protégé who feels as strongly about his or her goals as you feel about yours, someone who is as committed as you to making success a reality. Make it easy for the business friendship to begin. Reach out with an invitation to an after-work get together. By spending even an hour with a person, you'll be able to tell if you can make the person's career path a little less rocky. As a mentor, you'll share suggestions, offer advice, provide guidance.

TIPS

If you choose to accept the important role of mentor to another professional, there are some important considerations.

> *Allow your protégé to find his or her own road.* Your job is to point the person in the right direction.
> *Find out how your protégé learns.* Some people learn by being shown examples, others need to discuss various approaches, still others have to try things themselves to find out what works. When you figure out how your protégé learns, you can help him or her best by adopting that method of teaching.
> *Focus on strengths to improve weaknesses.* You'll want to help your protégé improve areas of weakness. To do that, focus on their areas of strength and show how those strengths can be used to improve weak areas.
> *Watch what you say.* Your words can confuse or wound your protégé even when they're meant to encourage the person. Think before you speak and reflect on how you would feel hearing your words spoken by your mentor.

You'll get a kick out of seeing your protégé progress just as your mentor enjoyed watching your advancement. You may also be amazed at one of the secrets of being a mentor—you often learn more than the person you're coaching. ■

How Lifelong Learning Contributes to Lifelong Success

According to President John F. Kennedy, "Leadership and learning are indispensable to each other." If you're under the impression that graduation means an end to all learning, you're mistaken. Successful people are lifelong learners. They know that learning empowers them and provides the means to move forward in pursuit of their careers and professional goals.

Unless you've chosen a career in which continuing education is mandatory, such as for keeping a license or attaining certain status in your field, continuing education will be your responsibility. If so, make a life goal right now to stay current in your industry.

Think of it this way. Businesses understand the need to enhance existing products. They tinker and tweak so that the product is more valuable and current with the latest technology. You are your own product, and you need to be the latest and the hottest one on the market. You need to know your field, where it's going, and how to keep up with it. Unless you keep learning—enhancing the existing product—people coming up behind you will have more current knowledge of your industry than you do, and you'll be left in the dust. You'll be an obsolete product that nobody will want.

If you haven't already done so, go back to Chapter 1 and the My Goals exercise and add lifelong learning to your list of long-term goals. Later in this chapter, you'll make objectives for accomplishing that goal. Follow up by adding something to your daily list of things to do tomorrow that will help you start reaching your objectives right away.

Ways to Become a Lifelong Learner

You can become a lifelong learner in a number of low-tech to high-tech ways, but the basic idea is to never stop learning. As a bonus, you'll also find that learning is much more fun when your purpose is to better yourself rather than just to be ready for a pop quiz. Here are some ways you can begin your lifelong learning.

Read magazines and professional journals. Whether delivered to your home or to your office at work, magazines and professional journals bring up-to-date information to you monthly or weekly. Almost every industry has at least one trade magazine. Choose one or two that are most relevant to your career and subscribe. Because periodicals are part of your professional development, you will probably be able to get your company to spring for the subscription costs. Once the issues start arriving, plan time in your schedule to read the features and columns.

Make the most of your reading time. First, scan the table of contents to see what's being offered in a particular issue then choose to read only the articles that interest you. Be selective. Don't think you have to read every journal from cover to cover.

Next, prioritize the articles you need to read. On the table of contents page, rank the articles you need to read in priority order with 1 representing the article of highest interest that you will read first. Prioritize the articles you need to read so that your reading supports specific areas of interest or current work projects.

Before reading an article, glance at the subheads within the piece which serve as an outline to the article. Scanning the subheads allows you to see the focus of the article to decide if it's really of interest. If an article lacks subheads, glance quickly through the text of the piece. That is often enough to help you decide if this is a feature you'll want to read in full.

After reading an article, put a checkmark next to the title in the table of contents. This shows that you've read a particular article and prevents you from starting the piece only to realize partway through that you've already read it. This is particularly helpful if you read a journal over a two- or three-week period of time.

Use a ballpoint pen or highlighter to note any items of interest for follow-up. Then on the cover of the magazine write the page number of the marked item. After you finish reading the issue, the page numbers will lead you back to those items you noted. Clip and file articles that you think will be helpful to you.

Also clip the articles you don't have time to read. Put them in a folder that you carry in your briefcase at all times so you can read while you're waiting. When you're having your car serviced or when you're left to cool your heels while waiting for a client, you can plow through an article or two. You could catch up with your reading while at the doctor's or dentist's office or during your lunch hour.

Articles you read in magazines and professional journals provide a great way to start conversations with others when networking. You can ask if the person has heard about the latest advance in an area. If the person hasn't heard about it, you can offer to send a copy of the article. People start paying attention to you when you know something before they do.

As you grow in your career, eliminate subscriptions to magazines you no longer enjoy or that no longer meet your continuing education needs. Put the funds toward magazines and journals that match your current level of professional growth.

Read books. In addition to magazines and professional journals, read the latest books on career success, motivation, and in areas of specific interest to you. Each chapter in this book includes a section called *Read All about It,* which provides suggestions to further your knowledge in given areas. Use those lists as starting points.

Before purchasing a book, scan the jacket copy to decide if the book is appropriate for your needs. Then read the table of contents to get an overview of the book's scope. You may be able to read only those chapters of special interest.

Plan your reading even if you're able to manage only one chapter a week. Read with a packet of index cards and a pen next to you, so you can take notes on your reading. For example, the concepts in Stephen Covey's book *First Things First* may be so meaningful to you that you capture his philosophy on the index cards and refer back to them during the week.

You can also use the index cards to refresh your memory before reading a new chapter. This helps you to get up to speed with the book before plunging into another chapter. In this way, you have continuity in your reading even though you may read each book in a piecemeal fashion.

Listen to educational and motivational audiotapes. Wouldn't it be great to have master sales trainer Tom Hopkins or motivational speaker Anthony Robbins sitting right next to you in your car as you drive to work? While these experts can't physically be in your car, their pearls of wisdom can echo from your cassette tape player.

Most bookstores and libraries feature educational and motivational audiotapes. They're excellent ways to keep your mind active with new thoughts and ideas, using time that would otherwise be wasted while you're stuck in gridlock.

Participate in Internet news and chat groups. Expand your networking capabilities worldwide by participating in Internet news and chat groups. Find these groups through USENET or LISTSERV directories available at your public library. When you become aware of and join a new group, monitor the postings for several days to determine if the group will meet your needs.

Participating in Internet groups has its own set of etiquette rules which you can usually find in a frequently asked questions (FAQ) file that you can download. Obey the rules, or you risk getting flamed or even worse—having your e-mail box stuffed with thousands of unwanted messages. Present yourself as a professional at all times, offer assistance to those who post questions, and be an active participant asking your own questions and posing discussion topics.

With some active groups, you may encounter a newsgroup directory logging hundreds of messages a day. Many of these postings may discuss conversation threads that hold little interest for you. Scan the subject headings and decide which ones to read and which ones to skip. Some Internet service providers offer a filtering device that sorts e-mail into separate category mailboxes. You can set up numerous category mailboxes and let the system do the sorting for you.

Attend seminars. Seminars are information-packed educational events. They can run for an hour, a half day, or a full day. Not only do they provide the latest developments in your field, they also serve as great events at which to sharpen your networking skills.

Find seminar announcements in magazines or professional journals, in your company's library or resource center, or through your professional associations. Once you attend a seminar, your name is added to the mailing list and other offerings are sent to you.

A typical seminar asks you to register in advance, and you receive an admission card to bring with you to the seminar site. There you'll receive an agenda and learning materials for the day. Before most seminars kick off, you have a chance to grab a beverage, then meet and greet other seminar participants. Bring plenty of business cards.

The seminar may offer a single information session or several breakout sessions from which to choose. If several sessions are offered during the same time period, most seminars make audiocassette tapes of all the sessions available for later purchase. If you're torn between two great sessions offered at the same time, you can attend the one that holds the most interest for you then buy a cassette of the other one.

An all-day seminar usually features lunch on your own, so during the morning sessions scope out someone you might enjoy going to lunch with. This is an excellent chance to do more one-on-one networking, and you might even become fast friends with your lunch buddy.

Most seminars offer certificates of completion at the end of the day, and some seminars even qualify for continuing education units (CEUs). If CEUs are applicable in your profession, ask someone staffing the registration table about qualifying for them.

Take continuing education courses. While seminars give you a taste of lifelong learning, continuing education courses provide a literal smorgasbord. You'll find courses in business, psychology, microcomputer technology, communication, financial management, recreation, hobbies, and more.

If there were courses at school that you wanted to take but couldn't fit into your schedule, you can probably find equivalents in the continuing education department of your local two-year or four-year college. The courses are non-credit so you don't have to worry about doing papers or preparing for finals, and the courses are also affordable.

A continuing education course that you should definitely consider is one in financial management or financial planning. Once you start earning money, you'll need to know how to manage your funds, set up a workable budget, and make sure you have money tucked away for retirement. Sure, retirement is years away, but experts will tell you that it's never too early to start planning.

If getting to a classroom course at night doesn't fit into your current schedule, don't worry. Many colleges now offer on-line courses that you can take at any time.

Check with the school's continuing education department for schedule information and ask to be put on their mailing list. That way you'll have a built-in system for reminding you at least once a semester that learning is an ongoing process and that you need to be an active participant. Use the following exercise to plan your lifelong learning goals.

YOUR TURN

My Never-Stop-Learning Goals

Purpose: To plan your lifelong learning goals.

1. Review your life goals and career objective and list in the space provided the education you will need to accomplish those goals.

_____

_____

_____

_____

_____

_____

_____

_____

2. Review your list of educational needs and prioritize them in the space provided, assigning 1 to the educational need with the highest priority, 2 to the educational need with the next highest priority, and so on.

_____

_____

_____

_____

_____

_____

_____

3. Create a section in your day planner labeled Educational Goals. Write your educational needs in this section and review it every week, so you can include in your weekly planning the steps to achieve your educational goals. Update this section as your goals change or as you realize the need for new educational goals. ∎

Building Blocks of Commitment to Success

Once you've determined what is important to you, you need to create building blocks of commitment to success. These building blocks are all the items you put into your daily planner that allow you to create your own successful life.

For example, you may decide that staying physically fit will help to create success in your life. Being in good shape will allow you to have more energy, stamina, and be more alert to take advantage of business opportunities. You may decide that running three miles every morning will help you to stay physically fit. Then create "morning run" as a building block of commitment into your daily schedule. Once the building block is in place, it will work as a reminder that during that time period every day you have a commitment to yourself to run three miles.

If family is important to you, create building blocks for family time. If your friends are important to you, create building blocks for socializing. If your spiritual life is important to you, create building blocks for reflection, prayer, and worship. Each building block of commitment that you create contributes to a strong wall of success that will stand the test of time.

Soaring to Success

Success is not measured by the amount of money you have in the bank. Success is a way of life that can be measured by the amount of good feelings you have every day and throughout the years. These feelings result from the progress you make in attaining your goals and becoming the person you set out to become.

Measure your success against your own vision of a fulfilled life. Whether your dream is to work as a self-employed entrepreneur or as a top-level executive in an international firm, you can measure success not by how far away you are from your goal but by how much of your time is spent in taking steps toward becoming the person you want to be. When you reach that part on your journey of a thousand miles, you'll cease creeping along the path and you'll soar to success.

Since you've taken the time to create a road map for your journey to success, stick to the direction you've outlined for yourself to follow. Continue to use this book as a guide along the way and as a reminder of where you started out and how far you've come toward achieving your dreams and living a successful life. Good luck and enjoy the journey!

And when you start soaring, as you will, keep in mind that the sky's your only limit!

ELEMENTS OF EXCELLENCE

Reread the sections of this book that pertain to those areas, paying attention to some of the additional book and Internet resources that can help you. Then create action plans for those areas that need some more attention.

Success is a process of small steps in the direction of your dreams. You can do it—one step at a time, one foot in front of the other. *Good luck!*

Read All About It!

Biehl, Bobb. *Mentoring: Confidence in Finding a Mentor & Becoming One*. Nashville, TN: Broadman & Holman, 1997.

Cameron, Randolph W. *The Minority Executives' Handbook: The Complete Guide to Career Success in Today's Culturally Diverse Workforce*. New York: Warner Books, 1997.

Carew, Jack. *The Mentor: 15 Keys to Success in Sales, Business and Life*. New York: Donald I. Fine, 1998.

Corbin, Bill, & Kim Corbin. *Getting, Keeping and Growing in Your Job: A Practical Guide to Success in the 90s Workplace*. Indianapolis, IN: Just Works, 1997.

Dilenschneider, Robert L., & Mary Jane Genova. *The Critical 14 Years of Your Professional Life*. Secaucus, NJ: Carol Publishing, 1997.

Dryden, Gordon, & Jeannette Vos. *The Learning Revolution: A Life-Long Learning Program for the World's Finest Computer Your Amazing Brain*. Rolling Hills Estates, CA: Jalmar Press, 1994.

Green, Gordon, W. *Getting Ahead at Work*. Secaucus, NJ: Lyle Stuart, 1989.

Haldane, Bernard, & Peter F. Drucker. *Career Satisfaction and Success: A Guide to Job and Personal Freedom*. Indianapolis, IN: Just Works, 1995.

Hendricks, William. *Coaching, Mentoring, and Managing: Breakthrough Strategies to Solve Performance Problems*. Franklin Lakes, NY: The Career Press, 1996.

Huang, Al Chungliang, and Jerry Lynch. *Mentoring: The Tao of Giving and Receiving Wisdom*. San Francisco, CA: Harper, 1995.

Kelley, Robert E. *How to Be a Star at Work: Nine Breakthrough Strategies You Need to Succeed*. New York: Times Books, 1998.

Kiewra, Kenneth, & Nelson F. Dubois. *Learning to Learn: Making the Transition from Student to Life-Long Learner*. Needham Heights, MA: Allyn & Bacon, 1997.

Shea, Gordon F. *Mentoring: How to Develop Successful Mentor Behaviors*. Los Altos, CA: Crisp Publications, 1998.

Sinetar, Marsha. *The Mentor's Spirit: Life Lessons on Leadership and the Art of Encouragement*. New York: St. Martin's, 1998.

Wild, Russell. *Business Briefs: 165 Guiding Principles from the World's Sharpest Minds*. Princeton, NJ: Petersons Guides, 1996.

Books I've Read

Use the space provided to list the books you've read in this subject area and to reflect on what you've learned from reading them.

1. _____

2. _____

3. _____

4. _____

5. _____

Internet Resources

http://www.onlinelearning.net

> This Web site provides information about on-line courses offered by the University of California Los Angeles.

> Use a search engine and the following key words to find information related to topics in this chapter: *mentors, mentoring, lifelong learning, adult learning, continuing education courses, on-line courses.*

My Favorite Internet Sites

Use the space provided to list your favorite Internet sites.

1. _____

2. _____

3. _____

4. _____

5. _____

Self-Assessment

After You Have Finished

Now that you have finished working through *Career Excellence*, check the progress you have made. Read each of the following statements. Then check Yes, or Maybe, or No to indicate whether the statement applies to you right now.

1. I can explain my most important values and beliefs to another person. ☐ Yes ☐ Maybe ☐ No

2. I have a dream for my future. ☐ Yes ☐ Maybe ☐ No

3. I have action plans for achieving my goals.
☐ Yes ☐ Maybe ☐ No

4. I can match my skills and interests to one or more suitable occupations by using career resources. ☐ Yes ☐ Maybe ☐ No

5. I have a good resumé and can write a good cover letter.
☐ Yes ☐ Maybe ☐ No

6. I am good at preparing for and undergoing job interviews.
☐ Yes ☐ Maybe ☐ No

7. I am good at understanding the needs of other people.
☐ Yes ☐ Maybe ☐ No

8. I am an active listener who respects the speaker and understands the speaker's message. ☐ Yes ☐ Maybe ☐ No

9. I am a good speaker, with good voice qualities and good command of standard English. ☐ Yes ☐ Maybe ☐ No

10. I use a planner and a To Do list to organize my time.
☐ Yes ☐ Maybe ☐ No

11. I can evaluate whether a job fits into my long-term professional goals. ☐ Yes ☐ Maybe ☐ No

12. I enjoy learning new things. ☐ Yes ☐ Maybe ☐ No

Review your self-assessment. Check the statements to which you answered Maybe or No. These statements show areas of potential growth for you.

Compare this self-assessment to the one you did when you started this book. Which areas reflect changes from Maybe or No to Yes? Great! You've made progress! Which areas are still marked Maybe or No? Those are the special areas you have to put more effort into. ▪

Success: Interview Notes

To help you achieve both interview and career success, the following Interview Notes have been included to use as you continue your journey toward a rewarding career path. These pages allow you to track your job search progression from *when* an initial resumé was sent to *when* you obtain an interview to *when* that job offer may be made. These journal pages also allow you to honestly critique your impressions of the interview in writing. Refer to Chapter 3—Success before, during, and after the Interview for further comments and suggestions on how to become a successful interviewer.

After each interview, go back and review your notes to see where you have improved. What were the results? Did you learn something new? What could you have done differently? Did the interview help you decide if you were the right person for the job? Keep these notes handy and review them often. In case your first job does not become a lifelong position, these notes will serve as a great tool for review in preparation for future interviews. They are yet one more step on your road to career success—right here, right now!

Interview No. 1

Date resumé sent: _____

Date of interview: _____   Interview time: _____

Company name: _____

Company address: _____

_____

_____

Telephone number: _____

FAX number: _____

Contact person(s): e-mail address:

1._____

2._____

3._____

4._____

5._____

Interview comments: _____

_____

_____

_____

_____

_____

_____

What went well? _____

_____

_____

_____

_____

_____

_____

What could be improved? _____

_____

_____

_____

_____

_____

_____

Interview follow-up: _____

Date thank-you letter sent: _____

Date of follow-up phone call: _____

Second interview date: _____

Third interview date: _____

Job offer date: _____

Acceptance of job offer date: _____

Start date: _____

Interview No. 2

Date resumé sent: _____

Date of interview: _____   Interview time: _____

Company name: _____

Company address: _____

_____

_____

Telephone number: _____

FAX number: _____

Contact person(s):   e-mail address:

1. _____

2. _____

3. _____

4. _____

5. _____

Interview comments: _____

_____

_____

_____

_____

_____

_____

What went well? _____

_____

_____

_____

_____

_____

_____

What could be improved? _____

_____

_____

_____

_____

_____

_____

Interview follow-up: _____

Date thank-you letter sent: _____

Date of follow-up phone call: _____

Second interview date: _____

Third interview date: _____

Job offer date: _____

Acceptance of job offer date: _____

Start date: _____

Interview No. 3

Date resumé sent: _____

Date of interview: _____ Interview time: _____

Company name: _____

Company address: _____

_____

_____

Telephone number: _____

FAX number: _____

Contact person(s): e-mail address:

1._____

2._____

3._____

4._____

5._____

Interview comments: _____

_____

_____

_____

_____

_____

_____

What went well? _____

_____

_____

_____

_____

_____

_____

What could be improved? _____

_____

_____

_____

_____

_____

Interview follow-up: _____

Date thank-you letter sent: _____

Date of follow-up phone call: _____

Second interview date: _____

Third interview date: _____

Job offer date: _____

Acceptance of job offer date: _____

Start date: _____

Interview No. 4

Date resumé sent: _____

Date of interview: _____ Interview time: _____

Company name: _____

Company address: _____

_____

_____

Telephone number: _____

FAX number: _____

Contact person(s): e-mail address:

1. _____

2. _____

3. _____

4. _____

5. _____

Interview comments: _____

_____

_____

_____

_____

_____

_____

What went well? _____

_____

_____

_____

_____

_____

_____

What could be improved? _____

_____

_____

_____

_____

_____

_____

Interview follow-up: _____

Date thank-you letter sent: _____

Date of follow-up phone call: _____

Second interview date: _____

Third interview date: _____

Job offer date: _____

Acceptance of job offer date: _____

Start date: _____

Interview No. 5

Date resumé sent: _____

Date of interview: _____   Interview time: _____

Company name: _____

Company address: _____

_____

_____

Telephone number: _____

FAX number: _____

Contact person(s): e-mail address:

1._____

2._____

3._____

4._____

5._____

Interview comments: _____

_____

_____

_____

_____

_____

_____

What went well? _____

_____

_____

_____

_____

_____

_____

What could be improved? _____

_____

_____

_____

_____

_____

Interview follow-up: _____

Date thank-you letter sent: _____

Date of follow-up phone call: _____

Second interview date: _____

Third interview date: _____

Job offer date: _____

Acceptance of job offer date: _____

Start date: _____

Interview No. 6

Date resumé sent: _____

Date of interview: _____   Interview time: _____

Company name: _____

Company address: _____

_____

_____

Telephone number: _____

FAX number: _____

Contact person(s): e-mail address:

1._____

2._____

3._____

4._____

5._____

Interview comments: _____

_____

_____

_____

_____

_____

_____

What went well? _____

_____

_____

_____

_____

_____

_____

What could be improved? _____

_____

_____

_____

_____

_____

_____

Interview follow-up: _____

Date thank-you letter sent: _____

Date of follow-up phone call: _____

Second interview date: _____

Third interview date: _____

Job offer date: _____

Acceptance of job offer date: _____

Start date: _____

Interview No. 7

Date resumé sent: _____

Date of interview: _____   Interview time: _____

Company name: _____

Company address: _____

_____

_____

Telephone number: _____

FAX number: _____

Contact person(s): e-mail address:

1._____

2._____

3._____

4._____

5._____

Interview comments: _____

_____

_____

_____

_____

_____

_____

What went well? _____

_____

_____

_____

_____

_____

_____

What could be improved? _____

_____

_____

_____

_____

_____

Interview follow-up: _____

Date thank-you letter sent: _____

Date of follow-up phone call: _____

Second interview date: _____

Third interview date: _____

Job offer date: _____

Acceptance of job offer date: _____

Start date: _____

Interview No. 8

Date resumé sent: _____

Date of interview: _____ Interview time: _____

Company name: _____

Company address: _____

_____

_____

Telephone number: _____

FAX number: _____

Contact person(s): e-mail address:

1. _____

2. _____

3. _____

4. _____

5. _____

Interview comments: _____

_____

_____

_____

_____

_____

_____

What went well? _____

_____

_____

_____

_____

_____

_____

What could be improved? _____

_____

_____

_____

_____

_____

_____

Interview follow-up: _____

Date thank-you letter sent: _____

Date of follow-up phone call: _____

Second interview date: _____

Third interview date: _____

Job offer date: _____

Acceptance of job offer date: _____

Start date: _____

Index

Mentors, 93, 157–160
    becoming a mentor, 160
    finding and working with, 158–159
Motivational audiotapes, 163

N

Names, strategies for remembering, 107–108
Negative beliefs, 9
Negotiating salary, benefits and perks, 97
Networking, 47, 49
    being open to opportunities, 104–105
    Benefactor Bingo, 109–110
    defined, 101–102
    formal, 102–103
    getting involved, 115–119
    informal, 102–103
    "network nag," 108
    planning encounters, 111–115
    promoting yourself, 106–115
    staying focused on goals, 108–109
    strategies for remembering names,
        107–108
    thank-you notes, 119–121
    volunteering, 116–119
    win–win aspects of, 103
Nonverbal communication, 130
Nonverbal cues, 130

O

Occupation. *See* Career
Occupational Outlook Handbook, 30, 73
Occupational Outlook Quarterly, 30
Office environment, 127
On-the-job attitude, cultivation of, 127–129
Organization, 144–146

P

Parkinson's Law, 143
Perks, negotiating, 97
Personal appearance, 48, 74
Personalized job search, 48–52
Personal qualities, 31
Personal shoppers, 128
Personal Vision statement, 22
Planners, 146–150
Portfolios, 64–65
Positive attitude, attaining and maintaining, 66
Positive beliefs, 9
Positive self-talk, 9
Priority setting, 144–146
Private employment agencies, 51
Procrastination, tips for combating, 21,
        138–139
Professional goals, 16–21
Protégés, 160

R

References, 62–63
Referral thank-you note, 120
Resource skills, 31
Resumés
    chronological, 59
    combination format, 61
    contents of, 53–58
    cover letters, 63–64
    functional, 60
    references, 62–63
    requirements for, 62
Robbins, Anthony, 129
Role-playing the interview, 89
Rosenthal, Julie, 129

S

Salary, negotiating, 97
Second interviews, 90
Self-assessment, 170–171
Self-beliefs, 12–13
Self-fulfilling prophecy, 9
Self-promotion, 106–115
Seminars, 164
The Seven Habits of Highly Effective People
    (Covey), 18, 103
Short-term goals, 16–18
Skills
    interpersonal, 32
    personal, 31–35
Speaking, 132–136
    effective conversations, 133–134
    on the telephone, 134–135
Statement of Personal Vision, 22
Strunk, William, Jr., 136
Success
    building block of commitment to,
        166–167
    defined, 1–2
    fear of, 21
    following path to, 21–23
    measuring, 167
    self-beliefs as basis for, 13
    soaring to, 167
Support network, creating, 158
Systems skills, 32

T

Technology skills, 32
Telephone
    contact thank-you note, 119
    interviews, 71
    techniques, 47–48
    tips for speaking on, 134–135

Notes

Notes

Notes

Notes

Notes

Notes

Notes

Notes

Notes

Notes

Notes

Notes

Notes

Notes

The Five O'Clock Club Series
Kate Wendleton

Celebrating 25 years as America's Premier Career Coaching and Outplacement Network for Professionals, Managers and Executives

Not your average job search guides, the Five O'Clock Club books offer advice from professional career coaches, with over 25 years experience advising and placing professionals, executives and career-changers. Kate Wendleton presents proven strategies for maximizing the interview; developing your career within your present organization; getting networking interviews with decision-makers; creating a resume; identifying the right career; and teaching methods for getting the perfect job. Numerous case studies make the content real, and easy to apply to *your* job search.

The Five O'Clock Club books give you the knowledge you need to:

- Develop your own "accomplishment statement" that you can use in your resume, cover letters, interviews, and more
- Create a winning resume that gets you in-person meetings
- Use the internet to effectively research your targets
- Secure informational meetings and networking interviews with organization decision-makers
- Gain power in the interview process
- Turn interviews into offers
- Use Kate's Four-Step Salary Negotiation Method
- Enhance your interpersonal skills to survive and thrive once you get the job

Mastering the Job Interview and Winning the Money Game
ISBN: 1-4180-1500-8

Navigating Your Career: Develop Your Plan, Manage Your Boss, Get Another Job Inside
ISBN: 1-4180-1501-6

Shortcut Your Job Search: The Best Way to Get Meetings
ISBN: 1-4180-1502-4

Packaging Yourself: The Targeted Résumé
ISBN: 1-4180-1503-2

Targeting a Great Career
ISBN: 1-4180-1504-0

Launching the Right Career
ISBN: 1-4180-1505-9

258 pp., 7 3/8" x 9 1/4", softcover

About the Author:

Kate Wendleton is a nationally syndicated careers columnist and recognized authority on career development, having appeared on *The Today Show*, CNN, CNBC, *Larry King Live*, National Public Radio, CBS, and in the *New York Times, Chicago Tribune, Wall Street Journal, Fortune, Business Week*, and other national media. She has been a career coach since 1978 when she founded The Five O' Clock Club and developed its methodology to help job hunters and career changers at all levels. This methodology is now used throughout the US and Canada where Five O' Clock Club members meet regularly. Kate is also the founder of Workforce America, a not-for-profit organization serving adult job hunters in Harlem. A former CFO of two small companies, Kate has twenty years of business experience, as well as an MBA.

www.delmarlearning.com

To place an order please call: (800) 347-7707 or fax: (859) 647-5963
Mailing Address: Thomson Distribution Center, Attn: Order Fulfillment, 10650 Toebben Dr., Independence, KY 41051